Myngath

Some Recollections of a Wyrdful and Extremist Life

Contents

o o o

Part One

Apologia

This work is a concise recalling - as an aural recollection to a friend, recorded and then transcribed - of some events in my wyrdful and sometimes quite eventful life. A concise recalling of some events (with much left unwritten), because it is the essence of this particular life, recalled, that in my fallible view is or rather may be instructive, and I have tried to present this essence in a truthful way and thus be honest about my failings, my mistakes, my past activities, and my feelings at the time.

As a friend who read a draft of Myngath commented, "It is a strange work because the supra-personal adventures gradually give way to very personal encounters..."

Which in many ways sums up my life - a hubriatic quest, by an arrogant selfish opinionated violent young man, which led to involvement with various extremisms and certain dubious activities; then, via πάθει μάθος, to a certain critical self-understanding often, or mostly, deriving from personal relationships; then to a rejection of all extremism; and finally to the development of a rather mystical philosophy - the philosophy of pathei-mathos - based on empathy and personal virtues such as compassion and humility.

A somewhat strange life, therefore; although, as I wrote in *Pathei-Mathos, Genesis of My Unknowing*:

> "There are no excuses for my extremist past, for the suffering I caused to loved ones, to family, to friends, to those many more, those far more, 'unknown others' who were or who became the 'enemies' posited by some extremist ideology. No excuses because the extremism, the intolerance, the hatred, the violence, the inhumanity, the prejudice were mine; my responsibility, born from and expressive of my character; and because the discovery of, the learning of, the need to live, to regain, my humanity arose because of and from others and not because of me.
>
> Thus what exposed my hubris - what for me broke down that certitude-of-knowing which extremism breeds and re-presents - was not something I did; not something I achieved; not something related to my character, my nature, at all. Instead, it was a gift offered to me by others..."

DWM
2010

∘∘∘

Early Years

Africa

My earliest - and some of my fondest - memories are of colonial Africa in the 1950s, where I, as a quite young child, spent many happy years. There are memories of travelling, with my father, in a car - with running boards and coach doors - along an upward road in the Great Rift Valley, and which road seemed to drop precipitously on one side, and which steep slopes held many a crashed vehicle, recent, and otherwise. There are memories of travelling to a European-only resort - by Lake Naivasha, I seem to recall - where there was a path down to the lake strewn with beautiful flowering plants, and where one could spent many happy hours while, in the clubhouse, elderly (to me) memsaabs would down their G&T's.

There are memories of playing in a shallow river near our dwelling in East Africa - no one around for miles - and of a family picnic by another, quite distant and deeper, far wider, river on whose bank was a wooden sign with the inscription *Beware of the Crocodile*. There are memories of going AWOL and walking - with the younger of my two sisters - miles and miles along a road, into the bush, and which road I had been told was off-limits to Europeans. We stopped once, as the Sun descended on that travelling day, to drink from our canteen of water and open the tin of beans I carried which we ate, cold (being even then of a practical outdoor nature, I had ensured I had a can opener). I seem to recall the Police - a European officer and his Askari - found us as dark fell, and I could not understand what all the fuss was about. Since everybody said we should not go there, I simply had to go and see what was there - which turned out to be just a road from somewhere to somewhere else.

There are memories of climbing trees - and falling from one and breaking my left arm. My younger sister - a companion on many such outdoor exploits - for some reason knew what to do, and made a sling from my shirt. Memories of - inadvertently I must add in my defence - smashing the glass counter of an Asian owned shop in the nearest village, whose owner demanded my father pay for the damage, which, of course, he did. I just had, you see, to try and juggle with some of the brass weights the shopkeeper used for his balancing scales. There is a memory of walking through some trees not far from my favourite stream and instinctively, with the panga I often carried while outdoors, chopping the head off a Cobra which, startled, reared up in front of me.

My interests were the interests I found by being outdoors. There was a colony of safari ants, for instance, that I chanced upon one day while out wandering, and I would spend hours watching them as their wide columns moved and marched across the reddish ground. Then there were the Chameleons I once, for some reason, long forgotten, wanted to find, and did, bringing one home to keep as a pet, which I did until I lost interest.

Once - for perhaps a year, or possibly more - I was packed off to some Catholic prep school, about which I remember very little except falling asleep a few times in lessons, and wandering off, into the grounds, when something interested me, or when I wanted to climb some tree. I do remember having a rather large magnifying glass and spending what seemed like many happy hours peering at things, outside. Perhaps I should have been in class - for I have vague recollections of being shouted at, by some adults, who seemed somewhat angry, and being somewhat bemused by all the fuss, as I recall on one occasion receiving six strokes of the cane for - something. Perhaps it was because - once, when the Sun reached in through a classroom window - I accidentally set fire to some papers on my desk using my magnifying glass. But, for whatever reason, I was soon and gladly returned to my parents (perhaps I got expelled), and life for me continued as before, mostly outdoors, mostly day-dreaming, and quite often exploring.

Far East

Africa faded into the Far East - as the decade of the fifties faded to a few years past a new one - and to life in what was then a rural area, not far from a lovely sandy beach by the South China Sea, and a service-taxi ride from the still then rather ramshackle and quixotic city of Singapore with its riverside cluttered with row upon row of Junks, and many of its streets festooned with stalls.

For some reason I soon had to go to school, every day, and by Gharry. At first, I loathed it - bumph to read, sitting at some desk, sometimes in the air-conditioned main building, and sometimes in the much better open-air Attaps in the grounds. Then - and quite why I do not now recall - I began to enjoy it. Perhaps it was the running track, where I loved to run, barefoot in the tropical heat; perhaps it was the young, gorgeous, blonde, English teacher who would often sit on one of the desks at the front, her legs crossed, and read to us some story, some poem, or some part of some classic novel. Whatever it was, I began to look forward to that school where by the end of the term, I was "second in the class", and top in several subjects, including (if my ageing memory is correct) English and Maths. I developed an almost insatiable appetite for knowledge, and began to read voraciously -

especially about Physics, Astronomy, and History. In addition, I learnt ancient Greek, and Sanskrit, and studied formal logic.

It was as if I had suddenly, quite unexpectedly, acquired a new way of seeing the world around me; as if some unseen force, some wyrd, some δαίμων, had shaken me and awoken within me certain dormant faculties. Or perhaps it was just the lovely tropical weather, the quixotic surroundings.

Whatever, through and with these faculties, with the knowledge I imbibed from books, a feeling, an insight, came to dwell within me. This was of our potential, as human beings; of how we might - and indeed should - change ourselves in a conscious way through overcoming challenges, as I had grown in strength and insight through running, training, through swimming often almost a mile out to sea, and through devouring knowledge. This insight became a vision of, as I have written elsewhere, "us freeing ourselves from the chains of this world and venturing forth to explore and colonize the stars. For I felt that it was this new freedom, brought by venturing forth to the stars, which would give us the great challenges needed to evolve still further, and naturally, into another type of being. And it was the pursuit of this ideal which I believed would create noble individuals and a noble, civilized, society...." [1]

By this time, both my sisters had left home, to be properly educated in England, something which I had wilfully resisted. One became - for some years - a Nun; the elder, a nurse at a teaching hospital in London, at a time when competition for such places at such a place was fierce, and required, I seem to recall, two 'A' levels.

As for me, I was enjoying my new life. Some years previously, I had taught myself to play chess, and now I began to play it at every opportunity, including at a local chess club (almost exclusively European, again if my ageing memory is correct) where I was the only boy. Some visiting Chess grandmaster was giving a simultaneous display - at the Singapore Polytechnic - and so off I went, one among perhaps thirty or so competitors, and one of only a few to manage to draw against him. And it was there, while wandering around, that I first saw a display of Martial Arts. It was almost balletic; full of seemingly effortless grace, and I felt at once that I wanted to be able to do that, to move so gracefully with the ability to generate, direct and control a certain physical power. So, youthful, vibrant, and arrogantly naive, I approached them. At first they - those Chinese men - seemed surprised, if not somewhat amused, that a young European boy (wearing white socks, khaki shorts, white shirt, and sandals) would be interested. But I persisted, and was invited to meet them a week later, at the place where they practised.

I remember that journey well. The service taxi dropped me near the Capitol cinema in Singapore city and, with a mixture of excitement and nervousness, I walked past that restaurant - much frequented by my father and I - that served rather good steak, chips, and fried tomatoes, for what seemed a long way. The young men were surprised to see me, although an elderly gentleman was not, and thus began my training. To be honest, I never became very good, and certainly no match for most of those there, and subsequently. But I doggedly persisted - so much so that, after many weeks, I was invited to join them on their usual post-session foray among the eating stalls by the river, and did not arrive back home until well past midnight, much to the relief of my mother who was on the verge of calling the Police.

Thus began my interest in and study of what, at the time, we colonial Europeans often called Oriental Philosophy, and thus was I invited to the rather splendid home - complete with garden - of one of the Masters of that particular Martial Art. From this developed an interest, both practical and theoretical, in philosophy, and religions, in general, including Hindu, Chinese, and Buddhist philosophy, religion, and practices, and Singapore was certainly a good place to learn about such things, given its diversity of culture, and replete as it was with Buddhist, Hindu, Taoist, temples and places of gathering. A good place, also, to be initiated, as a boy, into the delights of women; or, more correctly, learning of and from the delights of young delightful foreign ladies.

Fenland Beauty

Fade, to England on a dull, cloudy, cold day. An aeroplane; a long journey, broken by some days in Ceylon. The descent down through the clouds on the way to landing in England was quite bleak, for me. Everything looked so enervating, and for several weeks after arriving in England my only desire was to return to the Far East, or Africa. My father felt the same, and began to seek alternative employment in Africa, while I, to alleviate my boredom and inner bleakness, took to cycling the fenland country around and beyond the small village where we were, temporarily, staying. There was talk of school, but I artfully resisted, manufacturing a variety of excuses while I waited for my father to succeed. He did, some place further south in Africa than where we had lived, and near the Zambezi river, which rather interested me, although my initial joy on learning this was tempered by the reality of us - my mother and I - having to wait six months before we could join him, given the relative isolation of the place, his need to find us accommodation, and other sundry practical matters. The desire I had nurtured, for some time, to study assiduously, and go to an English University to read Physics, slowly dwindled; the dull cold bleakness of the English weather as water thrown upon that fire.

So I left home, at age fifteen, to lodge with a widowed lady in the nearby town, and spend what I assumed would be only six months at some College morosely and not at all seriously studying for 'O' levels. College work was easy, and at times boring, and I spent most weekends cycling mostly southwards, coming to enjoy the physical exertion, the landscape itself, and almost always taking a selection of books with me, carried in my saddlebag.

But there was something else, engendered by these journeys. A sense, a feeling - a wordless intuition - of not being apart from that particular fenland landscape, with its vast panorama of sky, its fertile soil, its often wide drainage ditches that, though hewed by humans, centuries of natural change had melded into being a part of Nature, there. It was as if this land - of small hamlets, small villages, scattered farms, with its panorama of horizons - was alive in an almost unique way.

I took to staying out on clear and moonlit nights. To cycling lanes by light of moon. There was a strange, eerie, beauty there, at these times - almost as if I, myself, was not quite real; that there lay a hidden world, an older, world, a far slower, world, where one might hear the whisperings of trees or hear the distant call of someone calling; someone long dead but not quite gone from the land, here; someone who did not belong in the other, modern, world that now edged this older fenland country.

There is no rational explanation for how or even why I met her. Perhaps - as I thought thereafter - it was she who met me, and meant to. Who somehow might have enchanted me to be there on that day at that hour in that year of my youth. As if she, also, was from, or part of, this other esoteric living land.

There were mysteries there that I did not then consciously fathom, but rather lived with and through, and which even now - over forty years later - I have only just begun to rationally understand as a natural and muliebral presencing of The Numen. Mysteries, perhaps, I felt then, of an ancient way never written down, and which no words, no book, could bind, contain, restrain, reveal. Mysteries of the connexion that links all Life together.

All I knew then was the occupant of that solitary small house along a narrow isolated lane near where the fenland waters, still, in those days, rose in some years to flood the land around and where a boat was kept, with daily life lived, if needed, on upper floors as in olden days. All I felt then, in the moment of that meeting and the hour beyond, was such an intense desire to stay as almost subsumed me. To stay - as one would stay stunned momentarily by the gorgeosity of some sunset, or by some vista suddenly chanced upon. No words sufficed, were needed, but we then idly talked nonetheless - I, leaning on my bicycle; she standing beside the broken fence that seemed to mark the inner sanctum of her sacred world.

It was not that I expected, then - or even hoped for - some kind of sexual tryst. But there she was, somewhat older than me, pretty in a comely way, standing, smiling, as I had slowly passed. It was not that I was lost and needed directions; a recent map was always carried in my bag. Not that I needed water. I had my flask of milkless Oolong tea. Not that I... But I stopped, nevertheless, dismounted, to slowly saunter back.

I have no clear recollection of what we said, for it is all now as a fading dream, remembered in the hour past rising from fitful unrestful sleep. No clear recollection of the two weeks that passed until I, unable to resist, ventured there again.

Mostly - as on that day of my first returning - we together just sat close to each other in the inner dimness of that well-worn dwelling. Sometimes a fire was lit; almost always there was tea. Sometimes we would walk together upon the land around. And we spoke, when needed not desired.

For it was a certain sensitivity that we seemed to share - a certain strangeness, a mostly wordless strangeness that I had previously not encountered; except, perhaps, in moments swiftly gone, as when one day the young, gorgeous, blonde, English teacher I still remember so well was reading to our class a poem and our eyes met, and it was if she somehow in some strange way then imparted in me not only her understanding of those words but also the feelings they engendered in her so that I, also, understood and felt the meaning behind such words. As if in that one short strange moment she had brought alive that work of Art so that it connected us, bridged us. So much so that for days afterwards I carried a copy of that poem around with me, and read it when I could to push open again that door that led to some distant different land. But, then, of course, the feeling faded, and some new interest, some new source of inspiration, came along; as - for me - that poem became surpassed, by others.

There was a walk, next time. Some talk about land, sky, Sun, Moon, rain, trees, insects, birds, and soil, and although I did not realize it then, I was learning; a learning, a species of learning, I once, many years later, strived to contain, constrain, reveal, with my own poor collocation of words:

Being the water: the Dragonfly above the water
I grieve of the road and the bridge of the road
Weeping in the wind
Because I am the Sun.

Being the river: all the river things
I feel the wounds
Inflicted deeply in my flesh
Because I am the dust.

Being the river-banks: the land around the banks
I am no-Time
Burning to cauterize my wounds
Because I am the world and all things of the world;

Being the wind: the words of the wind
I sorrow in my-Time
Knowing people who pass
Because they are my wounds.

Being my sorrow: the sorrow of wounded land
I sense the knowing turning beyond the pain
Because I am the water
Flowing with no end

There were other shared times, some when we simply listened to music. And then came that night when we two finally became lovers. Other such nights came; went, as the Moon, as the lady herself, cycled through several monthly phases.

It could have lasted; perhaps it should have lasted, for that is what she possibly, probably, wanted: for me to stay with her in that cottage of hers. But I was young, restless, impetuous, and in truth perhaps too selfish; too enwrapped in my own inner visions, dreams, desires; certainly, I was often impetuously youthful but not in love. Enchanted certainly, but no, not in love.

Thus arrived that day when I felt I had to leave, to never wilfully return - she stood there, by her dwelling, as I bicycled away, and although I did not know it then, she was only the first spinning of that muliebral thread that was to bind my diverse lives together.

Toward First Love

A rather generous allowance from my father enabled books to be purchased, and travel, by means of train, to anywhere that interested me, and so one day I travelled to London to visit bookshops, and the British Museum.

But that journey was fruitful in other ways. Arrogant and self-assured as I was - somewhat helped by my Martial Arts training - I spent some evening time in less salubrious parts of London, desirous of finding some suitable young lady to entertain me, remembering as I did such Singaporean trysts and wistfully recalling as I did that Fenland enchantress.

I did find such a lady, and, after a short taxi ride (which I of course paid for) we arrived at the entrance to a large town house in Chalk Farm. We had reached the top of that first tier of inside stairs (which led to her room) when some loud commotion broke out below. A man, shouting; a women's loud voice. From the stairs I saw a man push open the front door that a woman was, vainly, trying to close. He turned, shouted a few obscenities, and drew back his clenched fist, as if to strike the woman. He did not succeed. I cannot remember what I said, only that I said something to him after vaulting down that flight of stairs toward him. He replied with a vulgar epithet or two, and lunged at me. I simply turned, stepped sideways and used his own momentum to throw him to the ground by which time a huge man had arrived from some inside room to lift him, with remarkable ease, to his feet and almost bodily carry him out where he pushed him down the steps that led up from the pavement to that front door. The man lay motionless, briefly, there, then rose, slowly, to betake himself shabbily away, uttering curses as he did so.

I was thanked, by the lady he had intended to attack, and invited to join her for a glass of Sherry in her ground-floor rooms.

Thus began our friendship. Or, more correctly, relationship. Somewhat more than a decade older than me, with an enchanting if rather mischievous smile, she never once in the hours we spent together talking, that evening, mentioned the nature of her business, as I had no need to ask. It was all rather genteel, as she herself was, even though a trace of her local accent remained, and I found her quite enchanting, as, of course, she knew, drawing forth from me in those hours the then so brief story of my still so youthful life, and, our provided supper over, it seemed natural, an unspoken assumption between us, for me to stay the night with her. My stay became the following day, and then the day after that. There was a restaurant, of sorts, nearby, where she was known by name, and we spent a few hours there, eating a meal, and drinking wine, that neither of us paid for. I was introduced to her ladies, and to that huge man of the shaven head, who though rather grim looking had a gentle sense of humour. People - men and mostly well-dressed - came and went throughout most of the day and evening, and when my own self-appointed time came to leave, I did so with much reluctance and with a promise to return at the ending of that week.

I kept my promise, and it was to become the first of many such visits during those my early learning years. We had a simple, an uncomplicated, relationship, which was always honest, and I am not ashamed to say that in a way I loved her, in my then still rather boyish way, and - looking back, now - she almost certainly understood me far better than I then understood myself.

It is difficult, this understanding
Of my love:

I have to rise every morning
With the intention of our future
Moulded as some sculptors mould
Their souls around a form
That Will soon powers to a shape
In Time.

It is difficult, this sharing
Of each dream that makes her to journey
To the joining of our selves
And spills desire the way some music
Spills some notes to form the suggestion
Of some god:

There is no journey bribed by dread
No sea that sets the horizon
As the yearning of the dead sets
The seal to future Time;
There is no calling and no called:
No passing and no one passed
Since there is no you or I to understand
The laked reflexion of each moon.

But I forget, and need to remember
At each new beginning of each new
Dream which is the beginning of our
Love.

There are no words needed
As there are no excuses
For the failures of some Art:

It is difficult, this speaking
Of my love.

One weekend I particularly remember. Some hours were spent lazily strolling through what she insisted on calling *The* Regent's Park; some hours were spent listening to Jazz at some small club (she was a Jazz aficionado and very knowledgeable about that genre); and some hours spent at dinner in an excellent restaurant; and it was after midnight when we returned, by taxi, to her house. I remember then feeling pleased, and somewhat privileged, to be a part of her world - a young man who certainly felt, and behaved, much older than he was. Perhaps it was my childhood years in Africa and the Far East, perhaps my still then somewhat arrogant nature, perhaps my Martial Arts training, perhaps the manners my mother instilled into me and the liberal, rather laissez-faire, attitude of my father; whatever it was, I felt and acted quite differently from all the other young men of my age that I knew, some of whom, no doubt considered me elitist, arrogant, and somewhat condescending.

○ ○ ○

Ecce Ego Contra...

Political Initiation

One day - a Saturday - I was idly walking around the centre of London, sort-of heading for the house of my lady friend. Sort-of, because in those days, I quite enjoyed such walks, in still unfamiliar cities and towns. A chance to stroll past places; watch people pass by; become immersed in my surroundings. I had a good sense of direction, and seldom needed to consult the London map that I carried in the pocket of my Corduroy jacket. Indeed, it was often interesting to get a little lost - to find new sights, places.

In those days I still dressed somewhat conventionally, conservatively: Corduroy or Tweed jacket, flannel or Tweed trousers; sturdy brown walking shoes; even linen shirts with detachable collars held in place by studs inlaid with mother-of-pearl. Short hair, of course; and a rather heavy Tweed overcoat, for when the weather was cold.

Thus attired (*sans* overcoat) I chanced, on that day, upon some fracas in some street. Young men brawling. I had no idea at all what it was all about - but it seemed to me somewhat unfair, since one young lad was getting battered by several others. Without thinking, I waded in to help him. There was that exhilaration, again. That love of direct physical violence I had felt before. A few more young lads joined the melee, and then it was over, and so we went, quite naturally, to some nearby Public House to celebrate our victory. Their accepting camaraderie was wonderfully refreshing, and many hours were spent, drinking - and talking politics.

Not that I was then ignorant of their type of politics. Indeed, I had spent many of the previous months eagerly reading about nationalism, about National-Socialist Germany, and especially about Adolf Hitler, inspired by an account of the actions of Otto Ernst Remer, on that day in July 1944 during the Second World War. Such loyalty; such a sense of duty; such honour; such forthright warrior action.

To me, in the moment of my reading, then as after, Remer seemed the perfect embodiment of the warrior; of the type of person who might build the new society I had often theorized about - precursor as that society would be for our exploration and colonization of the stars. Now, it seemed to me, I had met a similar type of people. Or at least, those who could, given training, direction, guidance, purpose, be such people. Young; enthusiastic; who seemed to share something - if only instinctively - of my dream and who, like me, seemed to enjoy and welcome violence. They had a meeting, arranged for the following weekend, and I was invited and gladly accepted. I went to the meeting - and the "social" afterwards - and it was there I met someone who knew Colin Jordan, whom I had already heard of. Thus, it seemed logical, indeed necessary, that I contact CJ myself, which I did, by posted letter.

It was, perhaps, a propitious time. A new political movement had been formed, by CJ, and I began to seriously consider how the new society I had envisioned might be created. It also seemed to me then - and for a long while afterwards - that Hitler's National-Socialist Germany was, and should be, the archetype for such a new society: that NS Germany embodied most, though not all, the ideals I then saw as necessary to the creation of such a new, warrior, society imbued with a Galactic ethos.

For nearly a year I came to inhabit three quite separate worlds. My lady friend, in London, the world of occasionally violent but always interesting political activism; and my academic studies. Thus, I was fully occupied; enthused; alive; replete with my various ways of living, so that when the date for my return to Africa drew ever nearer, there really was no need to make a decision, for my lives seemed then inextricably linked with England. It seemed, then, as if it really was me against: you; the world; against everyone, except my political comrades and my lady friend.

During these trips to London, 'O' levels at College came and went, and I drifted into the Sixth Form. It was tempting to leave, and move to live and work in London, based with my lady friend, but the promise of Physics still enthralled me, a little, particularly as at that time the Apollo program looked it would easily achieve the goal that had been set - soon, perchance, there would bases on the Moon, and then on Mars. So I plugged away at Physics, without much enthusiasm, feeling it might be different at University when I would be free to undertake my own study, experiments, research. A feeling which led me to consider applying to King's College, Cambridge; which, after consultation with my teachers, I did and, probably due to their recommendation, secured and attended an interview.

Increasingly, however, my lives became a distraction from schoolwork, but I seemed to have some innate talent for mathematics and Physics and so - studying very little (some weeks, not at all) - I plodded on, trusting in this talent to get me through [2].

o o o

Facies Abyssi

University

Fast forward to a University in the north of England, and a still young student, who had grown well-trimmed moustaches and who, unlike the majority of other students, was always rather conservatively attired. My first term as an undergraduate had been a great disappointment following a Summer vacation of anticipation, and awaiting examination results.

No, wait - let us rewind, briefly, to that Summer vacation, after 'A' level exams were over. I had, perhaps rather foolishly, spent the weekends - and often the free days - of these examination weeks embroiled elsewhere. Attending political rallies, meetings, staying with political associates; and - more enjoyable - staying with my lady friend in London.

Possibly not so foolishly, since - in retrospection - I was, as became something of a habit, letting the Fates, wyrd, decide my fate when, as often happened, I vacillated between two or more options, waiting until a particular course of life seemed obvious, even to me. I had studied very little in the six months preceding those examinations, trusting to my talent, and busy elsewhere doing what, at the time and for almost a year before, were far more exciting and interesting things. So interesting and so exciting - so redolent of promise - that I even took the radical step of writing to King's College and withdrawing my application, feeling at the time and for quite a while afterwards that my future lay in London with a certain lady. A feeling which led me to impetuously send a request, via postcard, to the BBC radio programme Jazz Record Requests (a programme I knew she listened to), mentioning her first name and requesting - "with love from David" - a recording of the MJQ "with Milt Jackson on vibes". My request was successful, and I enjoyed a most memorable weekend in London with her. But then, months later, laboratory experiments led me to dream again of University; until - weeks or even days later - I began to desire again to move to London to stay with her... Thus, if I failed my examinations, I could not possibly go on to University, and the decision regarding my direction would be clear, fated.

'A' level exams over, I spent a lot of that Summer working, in a mundane job, for my allowance from my father never did, in those days, seem to meet all my needs, for I loved to treat a certain lady to the occasional 'long weekend away'. On the last day of Term, and slightly inebriated after a lunch-time session down the nearby Pub with friends, I had met one of only two girls (EH and JJ) in my Sixth Form. EH and I had flirted before, and I liked her, as I felt she liked me, but I had kept a deliberate distance, given my assignations in London, for to have yet another intimate relationship would have been for me, at that time, just far too complicated. But on that day - a warm sunny one, I seem to recall - as we passed each other outside the refectory I embraced her. She eagerly returned the embrace, and we kissed for a long time, much to the amusement of some other students, passing by, who knew us both.

Thereafter I did not see her again for a while, reverting back to keeping my distance, until I heard from a mutual friend that she was having some trouble with her landlord (like me, she had rented rooms for the Summer in our local town). Perhaps I misheard, or misunderstood the situation - but I thought I was informed that she had been threatened. Without hesitation I went back to my rooms to procure a weapon (one always keeps a selection handy). In this case, a pickaxe handle, and - suitably attired in the working type clothes I wore to work: jeans, brown leather jacket, heavy boots - I made my way through the streets to where he lived. My insistent knocking on his front door brought him out, and although I cannot remember what I said, I know he understood. I threatened him. I was just so angry; madly unthinkingly angry, full of rage, and prepared for a bloody fight. In that moment nothing existed except him and that, my rage. He was a tall and stocky man - bigger than me - but perhaps his own nature, or maybe something in my demeanour, my eyes, made him meekly agree to my demands. And so I left, still full of rage, and it was only as I was nearing my own rooms, somewhat calmer, that it occurred to me I was carrying what the Police would call an "offensive weapon".

Some days later, I was to learn that her landlord problems had been solved, and that she desired to see me, but I never did meet with her again.

So, fast forward again to University - that revealing of a part of my youthful character over - and back to that first Term, there. As I mentioned, I was so disappointed. I had gone somewhat naively believing I could study at my own pace, focus on topics that interested me, and do some practical experiments of my own devising. As it was, it was in many ways worse than school.

The lectures were tedious, rote-learning, affairs where one had to make copious notes and after which one was presented with a list of boring problems to be solved, each problem being of the type one might find in 'A' level examinations. Laboratory work as just as routine, even though one did have some choice as to what, of the listed experiments, one might undertake. Serious intellectual discussion, among the students, was at a premium - when it arose, which was rarely - and even the lecturers did not seem that scientifically curious. They had students to teach; or rather, certain parts of certain subjects to get through, every week.

One incident in particular made me seriously consider leaving, and involved a laboratory experiment. Toward the end of the first Term we were given the opportunity to devise and carry out our own experiments. I chose to replicate the Michelson-Morley experiment, having a particular interest in the theories that gave rise to this attempt to detect "the aether".

I was informed that such an experiment was really more suited to a Graduate, or Third-Year, student, but, of course, I ignored all the excuses and the advice that I was given as to why I should not try. Finally, I got my way, and was allotted a large part of one of the laboratory darkrooms. Suffice to say that it took me a while to set the experiment up, and even longer to tweak the equipment to get it ready: many weeks, in fact, despite spending many afternoons in the laboratory. I festooned my area with signs telling everyone not to touch the equipment. Then, I began to get some results. A few days later I returned, eager and excited, only to find that some lecturer had pushed all my equipment into one corner in order to set up some experiment for his students, thus destroying my weeks of delicate work. Not only that, I had "run out of time"; the darkroom really was needed by other students.

Strangely, I was not angry, just filled with an abyssal disappointment. It was as if some far distant apparently quixotic landscape which I had been eagerly travelling toward, for a long and arduous while, had at last been reached only to be revealed as ordinary, dull, devoid of any real interest at all.

Thus, gradually, my interest in studying physics waned, until - by the end of the next term - it has almost completely disappeared, replaced by increasing political activities, and a renewed desire to live and work in London. However, even though I never did any studious work, from that, my abyssal laboratory-moment, onwards, I still somehow managed to come second in mathematics at the end of year exams. There were various travels, and some trysts:

Here I have stopped
Because only Time goes on within my dream:

Yesterday I was awoken, again,
And she held me down
With her body warmth
Until, satisfied, I went alone
Walking
And trying to remember:

A sun in a white clouded sky
Morning dawn yellow
Sways the breath that, hot, I exhale tasting of her lips.
The water has cut, deep, into
The estuary bank
And the mallard swims against the flow -
No movement, only effort.

Nearby - the foreign ship which brought me
Is held by rusty chains
Which, one day and soon
And peeling them like its paint,
Must leave.

Here I shall begin again
Because Time, at last, has stopped
Since I have remembered the dark ecstasy
Which brought that war-seeking Dream

Meanwhile, my political involvements had intensified. I regularly attended political meetings, demonstrations, and activities, by various organizations, including BM and the NF, and at one such political foray I met Eddy Morrison and his friends. I immediately liked Morrison. He was enthusiastic, committed, optimistic, down-to-earth and quite *au fait* with National-Socialism. He also, at that time, possessed a certain personal charisma, and thus always had a few youthful followers who considered him their leader. One incident I remember well. He had invited me to join him and some of his friends on a day trip to Bridlington, an invitation which I accepted, and we ended up on the beach singing NS, and old BUF, songs.

A marvellous day, and I was genuinely sad when they dropped me off at my then place of University residence and went back to their city of Leeds, and it was not long before I joined them, again, for some political event or other. Morrison introduced me to his family, with whom I had a meal, and then off we went into the centre of his home city to raucously harangue some Communist paper-sellers and generally make a nuisance of ourselves. Morrison was far more experienced in practical street politics than I, and the more time I spent with him, the more it dawned on me that perhaps the two of us could not only make a name for ourselves but might, just might, be able to if not create the foundations of some new political force, then at least use an existing nationalist organization as means of gaining influence and power and thus begin to implement NS ideals.

It should be remembered that, at this time, the very early seventies, the NF regularly held large marches and rallies, all over England, with many of these marches involving violence, before, during, and after, and with many of these marches involving thousands of people. For instance, there was one march which I attended where those at the front had to physically fight their way through packs of Reds, with similar skirmishes occurring toward the rear. These were exciting times, and there really was a feeling, among the rank-and-file, that the NF was growing in such a way that, in a decade or more, it might be able to win or seize power.

Even CJ's British Movement was thriving, though in a much smaller way, and it was during this time that I came to act, on a few occasions, as CJ's bodyguard. Usually because the person who should have done that duty for some reason was not there. One of these occasions was at an outdoor demonstration - in Wolverhampton I seem to recall - when CJ stood haranguing the sparse crowd from the back of a Land Rover, while I stood in front, trying to look as thuggish as possible. Another of these occasions was an indoor meeting, where I stood at the front of the hall when CJ spoke, again to a small crowd, from the raised stage behind me and on which occasion I brandished a Shillelagh, which weapon the two or three, somewhat bored, Police Officers in attendance were completely unconcerned about. The Good 'Ole Days. On a few other occasions I simply accompanied CJ (walking slightly behind) when he walked toward and from some meeting place or assembly point.

Compared to all this, my life at University seemed, and indeed was, boring; dull. Thus it seemed natural, inevitable - especially given my friendship with Morrison - that I move to Leeds, and become involved with street-politics full-time. Which I dutifully did. As often in my life, it seemed as if the Fates revealed to me the direction in which I should go. Thus, and yet again, there was a certain period of drifting, by me, until a particular course of life seemed obvious, even to me.

My next year was a learning process. Learning about people; learning more about political propaganda; speaking in public; organizing and participating in street fights and demonstrations. That is, it was a learning of the Art of the revolutionary political agitator. I loved the life; I adored the life, and while domiciled in Leeds, in a garret (on Meanwood Road) appropriate to a revolutionary, fanatical, political activist, I still found time to visit my lady friend, in London.

One incident during my University stay may be worth recording. I happened to get to know someone there (who incidentally introduced me to the writings of Mishima) who was a personal friend of Martin Webster, and I met Webster on several occasions, one following some fracas at the University after he had been invited to address some meeting or other. On one of these occasions we had a discussion about political propaganda - a discussion which continued by several letters we exchanged over subsequent weeks. The essence of this discussion was to do with truth. I was of the opinion that if "our Cause" was indeed correct, and noble, as I believed, then we had no need to write or produce propaganda which distorted the truth in order to gain recruits, or make us and our Cause appear in some positive way. So far as I recall, Webster was of the opinion that I was being rather naive, and that, in practical politics, and to a certain extent, "the end justifies the means", something I then did not agree with.

Furthermore, it was during my time at University that I acquired personal experience of just how prejudiced some people could be - how they judged someone, for instance, according to their political views, or what they believed were their political views.

During my first few terms at University I had acquired something of a minor reputation as a fascist, helped no doubt by me handing out leaflets from the

Racial Preservation Society outside meetings arranged by various Left-Wing and Communist groups. This led to several people actively disliking me - even hating me - although they did not know me, as a person, and made no effort to do so. Thus, they judged me a fascist, they did not like fascists, so they did not like me; or, even worse, they believed that fascists were "evil" and/or dangerous and therefore should and must "be dealt with". What I found curious was that these people, who so irrationally prejudged people on the basis of their alleged or assumed political views, were often the ones who also loudly proclaimed that prejudice (including racial prejudice) was immoral. Thus, they were doing exactly what they were condemning in others.

I did, however, find one political person - who belonged to some minor Marxist-Leninist group - who understood this, and who thus took the opportunity to get to know me and with whom I had many friendly discussions about politics, and life in general. And it was he who - along with a few cultured non-political individuals - somewhat helped restore my belief that humans were, or could be, rational, cultured, beings. Perhaps I should add these few cultured non-political individuals - three young men and a young lady - were all (as we now say) 'gay'. Indeed, with only one exception, all my friends at University were gay, in those intolerant days (only a few years after the Wolfenden report) when such a preference, such a nature, was often kept secret because still regarded by the majority of people as reprehensible and somehow 'perverse'. As for me, I simply enjoyed their company; their culture; their sensitivity; and which culture and sensitivity was, or seemed to me at the time, rather lacking in most if not all the other students I met, studied with, or had occasion to interact with.

Excursus - Galactic Imperium

Since my discovery of National-Socialism, aged fifteen, I believed that NS Germany embodied the essence of - and could be archetype for - the type of warrior orientated and noble society that might make my vision of a Galactic Imperium real. I read everything I could about Hitler, NS Germany, and National-Socialism, and concluded - some time before what has been termed holocaust revisionism began - that the alleged extermination of the Jews during the Second World War was propaganda.

To me, then, National-Socialism seemed to embody everything that I felt was noble and excellent: a new, modern, expression of the Hellenic ethos which I had greatly admired since first reading, in Greek, Homer's *Odyssey* and *The Iliad* years previously. Thus my overriding aim came to be supporting and propagating National-Socialism, and aiding organizations which might prepare the way for a new type of fascist or NS State.

Furthermore, I really had come to feel a deep love for my ancestral land of England as I felt then an idealistic, and honourable, desire to help, to aid, those whom I regarded as my own people: as if all their problems could and should be solved by the emergence of a National-Socialist State; as if all that was required for Paradise to be created on Earth was the triumph of an NS movement and the practical implementation of NS ideals. Youthful exuberance and naiveté - perhaps.

In my understanding of NS I was greatly helped by Colin Jordan, who suggested I read certain books, including the works of Savitri Devi, who gave me many books, and loaned me others, who patiently answered my many enthusiastic questions, and who introduced me to many life-long National-Socialists, including some who had fought for, and given their loyalty to, Adolf Hitler, and one of my most treasured possessions came to be a signed photograph given to me by Major-General Otto Ernst Remer.

Even before I discovered NS and studied NS Germany, I had a vision of a human Galactic Empire, founded and maintained by a new breed of warrior-explorers, as I believed that we human beings possessed great potential and can and should change and evolve ourselves, consciously, by acts of will, and by overcoming, by accepting, great and noble challenges. Such challenges would reveal ἀρετὴ - reveal a person's true nature, and be the breeding ground of ἀρετὴ.

Thus, for me, discovering and learning about NS seemed fortunate, wyrdful - presenting to me the means to make my vision real.

As I was to write during my time living in Leeds:

"It is the vision of a Galactic Empire which runs through my political life just as it is the quest to find and understand our human identity, and my own identity, and our relation to Nature, which runs through my personal and spiritual life, giving me the two aims which I consistently pursued since I was about thirteen years of age, regardless of where I was, what I was doing and how I was described by others or even by myself..."

I further came to understand that in order to create the new warrior society, it was necessary to disrupt, undermine, destroy, overthrow – or replace by any practical means – all existing societies, and all governments, and that while electoral politics might be one way for National-Socialists to take power, direct revolution or insurrection was a viable alternative.

Therefore, with the dedication of a fanatic, I set about doing just that, ready, willing and prepared to use violence in order to aid and achieve political goals. For I then considered that sacrifices were necessary in order for these goals to be achieved, and that, once achieved, the violent struggle would have been worthwhile, even if it cost me my own life, or that of others. Thus, I placed some idealized vision of the future before my own personal happiness - indeed, my own happiness became the struggle for, and the practical realization of, that vision of the future.

Years of Ultra-Violence

Fade back to the English city of Leeds, in the first few years of that decade - reckoned according to a calender still in common use - called the nineteen seventies.

I was released from my first term of imprisonment, having been convicted of leading a gang of skinheads in a Paki-bashing incident, following some racial skirmishes in Wakefield, and I soon settled back into my life as a violent street-agitator. I had found prison a useful and interesting experience, made some good contacts, learned some new skills, and left with more money than I had entered, having run a racket inside, selling certain liberated goods.

In the weeks following this, I put some of my new skills to practical use, and began to put together the nucleus of a small gang whose aim was to liberate goods, fence them, and make some money with the initial intent of aiding our political struggle.

Suffice to say that this gang - more petty criminals than racketeers - was based in or around Leeds and consisted of some useful people. For example, someone who worked in a large Department store, and someone employed by British Railways who had access to large parcels and rail freight. Thus, these types of people had easy access to useful, saleable, goods. The railway employees would simply change the labels and documentation, so that goods were mis-delivered to a contact, and then sold on to a fence, while the store employees would arrange delivery of goods in a similar way, or one of our people would simply collect them in-store and boldly walk out with them.

For some reason I cannot quite now recall, Eddy Morrison became involved on the periphery of this group - perhaps he may have wanted a certain item, or two, which I, being his friend, said I could supply, etcetera.

For quite a while things ran smoothly - even when I happened to get arrested, convicted, and sent to prison (again) for a short while, for violence - until, one day in 1974, four or five Police officers from the then Yorkshire Regional Crime Squad (later to become part of the National Crime Squad), raided my garret in Leeds, and arrested me. Three other people in this small gang - including Morrison - were also arrested, and we were questioned for around six hours at the British Transport Police HQ in Leeds. Morrison and I were thrown into prison, "on remand", since it was feared that I would "intimidate witnesses" and that he was "my second in command" (which, unlike the first accusation, was not correct).

Having previously spent some time in Armley jail, being on-remand there did not bother me at all, and I soon settled back into prison life. Morrison, however, did not cope very well, and seemed genuinely surprised that I was rather enjoying myself. But, as I said somewhat humorously to one of the arresting Police officers, during one of my interrogations, "You get three meals a day, free accommodation, and there are lot's of friends around, so what's the big deal?"

It turned out that the Police had been "tipped-off" by one of those involved in this gang, because he had developed a personal grudge against me. The simple truth is that he had a violent argument with his girlfriend, she came to see me, and stayed for around two weeks.

> There is an ineffable sadness
> For your eyes betray that warmth, that beauty,
> That brings me down
> To where even my street-hardened Will cannot go:
> So I am sad, almost crying
>
>
> Outside, there is no sun to warm
> As yesterday when I touched the warmth of your breasts
> And the wordless joy of ecstatic youth
> Lived to suffuse if only briefly with world-defying life
> This tired battle-bruised body
>
>
> But now: clouds, rain-bleakness
> To darken such dreams as break me.
> For there are many places I cannot go.

So I let her go, suffused as I still was with a particular political vision and various political schemes. To add insult to the injury of the grass who betrayed us, when he finally managed to see his former girlfriend again to try and get her back, she compared him unfavourably, in one department, to someone else. Thus, his pride hurt, he began telling lies about me to anyone who would listen, claiming, for instance, that once he pushed me up against a wall and I pleaded for him to let me go.

Quite naturally, given my character at that time, I while in prison arranged for someone to sort this grass out, but this comrade of mine, on his way to do just that, was pulled-over and arrested on some other outstanding matter, held on remand and eventually convicted of a variety of offences, receiving a long prison sentence. Meanwhile, the grass had left Leeds and gone into hiding.

On learning of this, I considered the matter, wyrdfully, finally concluding that I should – then and on my release from prison and for the good of the Cause – put my political aims and goals before personal vengeance and certain 'criminal' activities and running a gang. Thus, I should strive to be idealistic, noble, and ignore – not seek to find - such an individual, and instead personally concentrate on politics, eschewing further 'criminal' activities to fund that Cause. Not that – to be honest - this decision to concentrate solely on politics was easy for me then, since it was very tempting to continue with such activities, which I did enjoy: the planning, the anticipation, the execution, the camaraderie, and the satisfaction of succeeding.

When this particular criminal case against me finally came to trial, all the more serious charges had been dropped due to "lack of evidence", and I was simply charged with "receiving and handling stolen goods", for which I was convicted and given a bender.

Fade, back to my political life in Leeds. While all the above was occurring, I was dutifully doing my duty as a street-agitator, and had been recruited (by JM) into Column 88, a clandestine paramilitary and neo-nazi group, led by a former Special Forces officer, which at that time held regular military training sessions with the Territorial Army, the volunteer reserve force of the British Army. According to gen received decades later, Column 88 was actually part of NATO's pan-European underground Gladio network, set up and trained to employ guerilla tactics against the Soviets had they ever invaded (as was still expected, in those days). But I knew nothing of this, at the time, and simply enjoyed being part of and training with Column 88. For C88 seemed to me to be a genuine National-Socialist group, devoted to comradeship and to the slow process of socially and politically infiltrating British society, with perhaps some possibility that, if the need arose (such as a Soviet invasion) we might "do our bit", as National-Socialists, and fight them.

Right from the very beginning it was obvious that C88 was a well-organized group, quite different from any other NS or nationalist group I had come across in the previous six years. For I had been instructed to wait in some obscure lay-by in Wiltshire, and was patiently doing so when several speeding vehicles arrived and proceeded - in an impressive manoeuvre - to surround, and block, the car I had been waiting in, with several very obviously fit young men exiting quickly from these vehicles.

I was further impressed when, later that day and in the house of C88's organizer (Lutz), I met many young National-Socialists from several different European countries. Here, I felt, was the spirit, the comradeship, of The Third Reich, of the Waffen-SS, of genuine National-Socialism, come alive again, something which, I knew from direct personal experience, was often so sadly lacking in the other NS group I had previously encountered.

While there was some military training - with weapons loaded with live ammunition - such as a night exercise in Savernake Forest when "we" had to take and overrun an "enemy" position, the real highlight for me of my years with C88 were the yearly Fuhrerfests when National-Socialists from all over Europe would gather in comradeship to celebrate Adolf Hitler's birthday. It was inspiring to know, to feel, that Adolf Hitler and his sacred mission had not been forgotten; that there were others - many others - in other lands who felt the same way and who understood, rationally or instinctively, or both, the essential goodness and nobility of National-Socialism itself. In addition, it was good to know that so many educated, seemingly well-connected, individuals in Britain were covert National-Socialists, for another impressive thing about C88 was its English members: professional, family, people, for the most part, who did not have a shaved head or a pair of 'bovver boots between them.

Indeed, I - although in some ways quite well educated - was probably the odd-one out: a rough almost fanatical street-fighter of many years experience who had been in Prison for violence and who had many other criminal convictions. That I, a hardened Nazi street thug with a criminal record, had been accepted into the home of L's wife and family - and into the homes of some other C88 members - was pleasing because it seemed to me to express the nobility, the folk equality, of National-Socialism itself.

In 1973 - just before I was recruited by Column 88 - Colin Jordan invited me to his then home in Coventry. Naturally, having great respect for CJ, I accepted and was to find, on my arrival, that a meeting of the inner Council of CJ's British Movement was taking place. After a short wait, I was invited to address them, which I did, answered a few questions about tactics and strategy, and then had to wait for a while in another room, which CJ used as his office. Invited back, I was informed that they had decided to co-opt me onto the Council, something I had not expected. Asking for time to consider the matter, I left to travel back to Leeds. For reasons I cannot now quite recall, a few days later I wrote to CJ declining the offer probably because I was already then thinking of forming my own, more violent, political organization.

In December of 1973, I finally managed to convince Morrison that we two, with our good ally Joe Short, should form a new political, more active (that is, more violent) and openly pro-Nazi, movement.

Thus the National Democratic Freedom Movement (NDFM) was born, which was to have a brief, if exceedingly violent, existence, with Morrison as leader. Our intent was to build a revolutionary street movement, and so for seven or so months we held public meetings, organized demonstrations and protests, and generally had a jolly good time (or at least, I did) in pursuit of gaining members and propagating National-Socialism under cover of nationalism.

As John Tyndall later wrote in his *Spearhead* magazine (April, 1983):

> " The National Democratic Freedom Movement...concentrated its activities mainly upon acts of violence against its opponents. Before very long the NDFM had degenerated into nothing more than a criminal gang."

Among the highlights of that NDFM year, for me, were the following.

I smashed up (with one other NDFM member) an anti-apartheid exhibition, in Leeds (twice). I gave vitriolic extempore speeches at public meetings (some of which ended in violence when our opponents attacked). I waded into some Trade Union march or other, thumped a few people then stole and set fire to one of their banners (arrested, again). I arranged a meeting at Chapeltown, in Leeds (the heart of the Black community then) at which only five of us turned up, including Andrew Brons but not including Morrison. We faced a rather angry crowd of several hundred people, who threw bricks, stones, whatever, at us, and we few walked calmly right through them to our parked vehicles, and rather sedately drove away, our point made. No one said we could do it.

I spoke extempore at Speakers Corner in Hyde Park for around a half an hour to a crowd of over a thousand (it ended in a brawl) - the only person from the extreme Right to speak there since the days of Oswald Mosley. At the brawl, one of our stewards was arrested, and - the fighting over - we regrouped to march toward Downing Street, after which we all went our separate way (I quite naturally went to see and stay the weekend with my lady friend in London).

Finally, toward the end of that Summer, a meeting we had arranged on Leeds Town Hall steps resulted in a mass brawl when the crowd of around a thousand attacked us, after I had harangued them for around half an hour. Several Police officers were injured as they tried to break up the fights. I was arrested (again) but soon was granted bail. Morrison became somewhat disillusioned, as I was by the attitude of many of those involved with the NDFM, and so I spent the time before my trial occupying myself with various travels around England and the NDFM simply slid into obscurity, a political failure - although, at least for me, it had proved to be an exceptionally valuable learning experience.

When my case came to trial, at Leeds Crown Court [3], I was accused of having "incited the crowd" and generally held responsible for most of the violence. I was found guilty of various so-called Public Order offences, and given several fines. What rather disgusted me after the trial was that several so-called comrades - including if my memory is correct, Morrison - having appeared at witnesses at the trial, collected between them witness expenses sufficient to pay my fines. But not one of them offered to do this, and I was not going to ask.

So, since I had no intention of paying the fines, I left Leeds.

Facies Abyssi

For well over a year I evaded the consequences of not paying my fines, living as a vagrant, then in a caravan in the fenland. Writing poetry. Musing on life; reading the collected works of Jung and Toynbee; studying religions, including Buddhism. Listening to numinous music. And so on.

> Crows calling while sheep cry
> By the road that shall take them
> To their death:
>
> I sit, while sun lasts
> And bleeds my body dry
> In this last hour before dark

On a day when a warm wind
Carried the rain that washed
A little of this valley
Like the stream washes
My rock:

There are no trees to soften
This sun - only heather and forn
To break the sides of the hill;
I cannot keep this peace
I have found -
It seems unformed like water
Becomes unformed without a vessel
A channel or some stream:
It cannot be contained
As I contain my passion and my dreams.

There are no answers I can find
Only the vessel of walks in hills
Alone
Whereby I who seek
Am brought toward the magick peak
That keeps this hidden world
Alive

I even spent some time in a Buddhist monastery. But the Police eventually caught up with me, in my caravan, and I was arrested, and sent to prison (yet again). But this time for only six months.

My previous experiences of "being inside" were useful when I was sent back to prison. Luckily, I was assigned one of the best prison jobs, Library red-band (even though I was serving a short sentence), which job meant that I had a single "peter", that I took over a few rackets, and was left pretty much to my own devices in the library. One of the rackets revolved around goods smuggled in; another centred on porn magazines ordered by the nonces on Rule 43 and which magazines had a strange habit of disappearing or not being delivered or getting handed round other cons for a small fee; another racket involved goods being liberated from certain prison stores.

At that time, prison life was a delicate balance, so I occasionally helped out someone who also had some rackets (centred around gambling) by getting a few people to "carry" tins of tobacco for him. Overall, a reasonable time, which meant that my release date seemed to come around quite quickly.

On release from prison, I was undecided, for a while, about what I should do.

I visited my lady friend in London, who by then had larger premises and a more select clientèle, and after travelling around for a while as an itinerant, I drifted back to live in Leeds. Morrison [4] had some minuscule and new political organization, was still talking the same rhetoric, and still unrealistically dreaming of obtaining political power in a decade or so. At least he was, outwardly, consistent.

As for me, for over five, often violent years, radical street politics had been an important part of my life - often, the most important part; and I had dedicated myself to the struggle, undeterred by prison. But my naivety, idealism, and optimism had all but faded away. For experience had revealed to me that the honour, loyalty and commitment to duty I expected from fellow political comrades was often absent, and that the leadership of all NS, all pro-NS groups and even all of our kind of nationalist organizations was woefully bad; un-charismatic and incapable of inspiring the loyalty required. Instead of idealism, loyalty and honour there were continual feuds, continued disloyalty, and little or no honour, manifest most often as this dishonour was in the spreading of malicious rumours behind people's backs.

My time away from Leeds - over a year, before my return to prison - had taken me back to those Fenland feelings of the late sixties. In particular, my solitary time as an itinerant had brought me close to Nature in very simple and unaffected way, so that there gradually arose in me a certain wordless feeling of dissatisfaction with modern life that had nothing whatsoever to do with my political beliefs, dreams or aspirations. In fact, nothing to do with any ideology, or, at that time, with any religion I had studied or personally experienced. Instead, it was interior, direct, personal - one individual, alone, who felt some relation with Nature, with the Cosmos, and it is true to say that this wordless feeling, and my memories of life close to Nature, rather haunted me when I returned to live in Leeds.

I just did not feel I belonged there, anymore. I yearned - for something; as one might yearn for a young lady seen briefly, spoken to briefly, whom one met on some travels, and whose presence, whose aura, whose scent, whose features, whose promise, lingered when she was gone; lingered so much, so numinously, that one regretted not running after her and blurting out some excuse to be with her, again. I yearned - for those intangible wistful moments of a wandering life:

Wine

Stale
I once drank you

Knowing no difference because of herbs.
She held me, her cunning hands
That did not wish
Nor offer the warmth that snared my soul:

The wine was
Intoxicating our senses
But only I was drunk:
She laughed.

I needed rest
Dreaming marriage under sun -
Until bright morning came
When she, alas, changed
Her form in the reality of the room
And I was left to walk with my sack
Down the dusty track
Past a grove of sun-burnt trees
Toward those distant hills:

And yet the white-washed house was only
One step
Along my Way.

Perhaps it was that hot, dry, Summer of 1976 with its week after week of clear blue skies; perhaps it was some inner un-thought of satisfaction with my own subsuming political aims; some surfacing, some re-emergence, of that youthful desire to know, to understand, myself, Life, the Cosmos. Perhaps it was the feelings that gave rise to the many poems I had written in my wanderings; poems such as the compilation *Gentleman of the Roads*, and the poem *Clouds in the Sky*. Whatever the cause or causes, I found myself increasingly desiring to be alone; increasing desiring silence, both external and within; increasingly desiring to somehow in some way reconnect myself with that other older world that my political machinations and activities seemed to have almost totally obscured.

Two wyrdful things conspired together to seal my fate. The first was the music of JS Bach, especially some Cantatas. The second was a strange encounter at an old Parish church on the edge of the fenland in King's Lynn.

The new female companion I had acquired on my return to Leeds shared my love of classical music, and I went to many concerts and performances with her. At one, during a performance of Bach's *Erbarme Dich*, I began to cry, silently: silent tears of unknowing, of sadness and of joy.

Not longer after, I ventured to return to visit a friend in Norfolk, and - somewhat early for the bus that would take me near his dwelling - I passed some time by perusing what seemed an interesting Church, having, at that time, a minor interest in architecture. Somewhat tired after a long journey, I sat for a while in some pew. Then this young man, in clerical garb, passed in front of the altar to briefly turn toward me, and smile. There was such gentleness, such purity, in his face, his demeanour. And then he was gone, out of my view, toward what I assumed, then, was some door. It was as if, in that moment, I knew he might have answers to some questions which I had been pondering for some days before, and so, instinctively, I rose to follow him only to find a solid wall where he had disappeared from my view, and it was only later, days later, that I discovered that once - centuries ago - there had indeed been a door there, and that the Church itself had been part of a medieval Priory.

He was so real; nothing in his appearance, his manner, to suggest a ghost, an apparition; and for weeks afterwards I tried convince myself that my tiredness, the unanswered questions in my head, had somehow in some way contrived to present me with some illusion, some delusion. But a vague feeling of unease remained - for there was that numinous face, that smile; that gentle presence radiating an inner contentment and a certain mystical peace.

My unanswered questions had to do with existence - with life - after our mortal death, and with the allegory of Jesus of Nazareth. An allegory I had felt, touched, when a performance of Bach's Matthew Passion had surprised me, had impinged itself, not long before, upon my psyche, bringing once again from one momentous passage, those silent tears of my unknowing.

The truth I felt, the truth which thus became so revealed, was that I did not know; that I did not have all the answers; that I had begun to doubt everything that for years I had so passionately, even fanatically, believed in. The truth that maybe, just maybe, I might not be able to find all the answers by myself, unaided; that maybe, just maybe, there was someone out-there, or something, who and from which I might learn, who and which might guide me toward a deeper, a better, understanding of myself and this world. That maybe, just maybe, in that particular allegory I might find some answers.

Thus there arose slowly in me after these events some desire to know about a certain, a particular, a quiet and inner way of life which I felt might be able to provide me with some answers, which might in some way connect me - reconnect me - to a beautiful, purer, way of life.

For a long time I had, in pursuit of some ideology - what I would later describe as a causal abstraction - controlled an aspect of my character: my almost naive sensitivity, my empathy, my rather boyish enthusiasm. But now this aspect came again to live, on a daily basis, so that I, perhaps rather foolishly, took to walking the streets of Leeds barefoot, and smiling like some village idiot; so pleased, so very pleased, to be alive; so happy with the blueness of the sky, the warmth of the Sun, the ineffable beauty of life itself. As if I was detached from myself, not really some young man named Myatt but rather

> A falling leaf turned Autumn brown
> Following the wind of the moment:
> Neither clinging to, nor striving against,
> The force of existence ever a dream in the end

For several weeks my plan became to return to an itinerant life, and thus became a kind of wandering poet, some sort of modern Taoist: a Way of Life familiar to me from my study of Taoism and my practical involvement with a Taoist Martial Art. But it seemed as if the wyrdful Cosmos had a rather different plan, for one day I decided - for reasons I cannot now recall - to borrow a bicycle belonging to a friend and head out for a week's holiday in the English countryside. A train conveyed me part of the way, and - the weather still hot, dry, and sunny - it was a pleasure to be away from the city, and I became as a schoolboy again for whom nearly every mile pedalled was an adventure.

There were stops for food, water - and a few overnight stays, often in some field beside some hedge. It did not matter, for I was still young, healthy, and quite strong.

After several days I came to be cycling down some narrow lane. To my left, a wooded hill of conifers; on my right, fields flowing gently upward to where a collocation of buildings were gathered just below a swathe of deciduous trees. The largest building somewhat - and I thought incongruously - resembled a French château, and so, intrigued, I cycled on to take a turning which I hoped might lead me toward it.

It was a monastery, and, leaving my bicycle propped up against a nearby tree, I wandered around. The door to the Abbey church was unlocked and I went inside. The cool quietness was slightly perfumed with incense from some recently ended Mass and a feeling of immense relief came over me as if I had, finally, come home. Words, scenes, emotions, scents, memories from a Catholic childhood lived within me once again, and it was so peaceful, so blissfully peaceful, sitting there, in the nave, that Time ceased to have any meaning or cause me any feeling as it trundled on in that other world, outside. Such stillness I had not thought possible came to keep me still.

I have no idea for how long I sat there, unthinking, and it was only when some activity in the monks choir beyond, behind, the altar distracted me that I remembered who and where I was. Then - their noonday prayer, chanted.
.

Suffice to say that when I returned to Leeds, soon afterwards, I immediately wrote to the Guestmaster of the monastery enquiring about a weekend visit. Some weeks later, I was there, at home, again. A weekend became a week; a certain request; an excited and nervous return to Leeds; and then that day when, with my few belongings, I ventured forth to begin my new life as a monk.

> Sun, broken by branch, seeps
> Into mist
> Where spreading roots have cracked
> The stones, overgrown, perhaps,
> For an hundred years
>
> From a seed, flesh fed, the oak
> Sheltering
> Mary
> Relict of William
>
> And a breeze, stirring again
> This year
> The leaves of an Autumn's green gold

ooo

Part Two

Sensus Internus

Into The Light

Monastic life was, quite obviously, a complete contrast to the violence, the carnal indulgence, the political activity, the time spent in prison, of my previous years, and my first month in the monastery did not come as a surprise. I enjoyed it.

Like prison, there was a daily routine, and I soon adapted to it. Or, rather, I embraced it joyfully. Rising, in those years (I think they have gone a bit soft, now), at around half past four in the morning to - without breakfast - spend two hours and more in the monks' Choir stalls of the Abbey chanting Matins followed by Lauds and followed by Conventual Mass. The breakfast, in the refectory, was substantial. Then there was work, study, until past Noon, and Choir again for prayers before lunch, and at which meal one of the monks would read a religious text to us while we ate in silence, using a particular monastic sign language if for some reason we needed to communicate between ourselves, such as 'please pass me the butter'. An afternoon of manual labour followed, with a short break for cups of tea; more work or study until the hour of Vespers, sung in Latin, with the monks precessing from the cloisters, in cowled robes, into the Choir. Then the last meal of the day - supper - followed by an hour or so of "spiritual contemplation" and then onto the last prayers of the day, Compline. It was now not long after nine o'clock in the evening, and one was, quite understandably, somewhat tired, and so went to bed, in my case a cell (a small room with a small window) on the very top floor of the Abbey on what was called the Novices Gallery. Interestingly the only heating in these monastic cells - apart from the rooms of the Abbot and Prior, who had fireplaces - were hot water pipes running along the outside wall (no radiators). Of course, by the time the steam-generated hot water reached our pipes at the top, they were somewhat colder than in the rooms on the floors below.

Suffice to say, we were kept, busy, occupied, and I seemed to fit in quite well. It was also remarkably easy to forget about the outside world - and if something deemed really important happened in the outside world, one of the monks would pin a typed summary - a very small summary - of the event on the noticeboard in the cloister, which in practice meant once every month or so. Mostly though, the notices there were mainly about ecclesiastical matters - the Pope on a visit, somewhere; or a forthcoming visit to the monastery by some Bishop or other. A few of the monks were endearingly eccentric; for instance one had a fondness for eating - raw - the little mushrooms that occasionally sprouted, at certain times of year, on the lawn outside the calefactory window; another would - with the soles of his well-polished patent leather shoes - crunch a cockroach or two on the floor of the refectory before they could scamper away when we after hours of prayer went to eat our breakfast...

Weeks became months, and one of my jobs involved me working in the monastery library - a beautiful large place, of stone-mullioned windows (most of which did not open or had not been opened in decades), row upon row upon high row of dusty old books (many in Latin), large collections of manuscripts, and a quiet quietude that propelled one back into medieval times. It was as if the modern world - with its haste, its technology, its electricity - no longer existed, and, my allotted tasks accomplished, I could browse, and settle down to read. And if by some chance (and as occurred quite often) I came across something I could not understand - some passage in Latin, or Greek, for instance - there was always someone, some scholarly monk, who could not only explain it to me but also place it in context, and who more often than not was willing to discuss the matter in great detail.

The monastery provided me with many opportunities, to study, to learn, to discipline myself, to acquire a new perspective on life, and - for a while - I did believe I might have a vocation.

But after many months I became somewhat restless, and - obtaining permission to leave enclosure - I began running down the lane from the monastery toward the small wood-enclosed lakes about a mile and half distant. Not that I had "running shoes" or anything like that - only some old plimsolls obtained from The Dive. The Dive was in the basement of the monastery, run by one of the monks, and was where one might find some item one might need - a pair of sandals perhaps; or a shirt. Possibly even a tennis racket; an umbrella; or a hat if one was out in the Sun in the beautiful, secluded, wooded Monks Garden above the monastery, on the slope of a hill. Naturally, most if not all these Dive items were second, or third, or fourth hand, "donated" by monks, or their relatives, or someone else, and some items had been there - borrowed, and then returned, and sometimes repaired - for perhaps a half a century or more. A veritable emporium, and if something one needed was not in The Dive - which was rare - it could be obtained, given some time.

This restlessness abated, a little, during those times I spent with four people there, three of them monks. The first was an older, jovial, monk, who possessed a great knowledge of Buddhism, especially Zen Buddhism, and who, in fact, had spent some years as Prior of a Zen monastery in Japan. We had many interesting discussions, about Buddhism, about Catholicism, about religion in general. The second person was a Greek scholar - a layman who lived in the monastery - and I seem to recall that he kept a card, filed among voluminous wooden card-indexes, for every single verse of The Odyssey, and which card contained, in his scholarly handwriting, the text in Greek, his translation, and some of his notes. The other two were younger monks - older than and senior, in monastic terms, to me - who had an interest in the more arcane aspects of religion, and especially of Catholicism, and we three would spend hours upon hours discussing mysticism, esotericism, and religion in general, even though, according to certain monastic rules, I should not have been associating with them as much as I did.

One rather humorous incident during my time in the monastery is worth recounting. I was asked, by the Abbot, to spend some weeks in Dublin where some University research project was underway, funded (I believe) by several monasteries, into vocations: what motivated young men to become monks; what might the monasteries do to attract more vocations, and so on. Why I - with my past - had been chosen to take part I found somewhat strange; or, perhaps, I had been chosen because of my past, a past known in full to both the Novice Master and the Prior. Whatever the reason, it meant flying from the nearest airport to Dublin, staying in a Presbytery near Phoenix Park and attending the University every day.

So, there I am, at the airport in England, travelling under my real name [5], waiting with other passengers in the departure lounge to board the aeroplane, when I am taken away, by two Special Branch Police officers, to be "interviewed" in a nearby room. Obviously they - or some other official - had recognized my name, or I was one some official Special Branch watch list. They asked why I was going to Dublin - and I explained where I was living, and why, and that the Abbot had selected me to take part in some research at the University. One of the Police officers then said that they would "check out my story" - and he duly returned, not long afterwards, and said I could go.

It was only on my return to the monastery, over two weeks later, that I learnt what had occurred. The Police officer had telephoned the monastery and enquired if there was a certain DM who lived there and what he was doing.

One of the older monks happened to answer the telephone, and - in his schoolmasterish way, as though lecturing a schoolboy - confirmed my story, making some remark to the effect that he would be happy to ask the Abbott to telephone the Chief Constable, at which point, as he with great amusement later recounted to me, the Police officer said, somewhat sheepishly, that no, that would not be necessary.

Fundamentally, however, although I generally - most days - enjoyed the life immensely, three things surfaced to unsettle me, more and more, even though for quite some time I fought against them, strengthened as I was by certain numinous aspects of monastic life. For example, by the office of Compline and the singing of the beautiful Latin Salve Regina after which most of the monks, myself included, would go the kneel in silent reverential prayer on the bare stone floor in front of a centuries-old statue of the Blessed Virgin Mary. For example, the short contemplative time between Matins and Lauds when it was peaceful, so blissfully peaceful, to wander outside in the darksome quiet or just sit still in the Choir and sense the centuries of numinous longing, joy and hope, that had seeped forth in prayer from places such as this.

The first - and for me perhaps the most important - of these three unsettling things was that I missed women. I missed everything about them - carnal relations, naturally, but also their presence, their touch, their embrace, their scent, their sensitivity, their gentleness, that intimate often wordless sharing that arises from a passionate, lustful, sharing relationship. In brief, I missed - and desired - the essence of women. Or at least, the essence of a certain type of women that I had become familiar with: the empathic, cultured, refined, well-mannered, passionate lady with whom and through whom one could be part of and explore a numinous reality.

The second was my combative nature - I loved to dispute, to argue, and many of the noviciate lectures degenerated into discussions between me and the senior monk trying to instruct we few novices. I argued about and disputed what the other novices thought were the most trivial things - for instance the exact meaning of certain words, and one discussion, in our course on New Testament Greek, about the meaning of the word λόγος, went on for hours. Eventually, in a rather nice way, I was told I was being somewhat disruptive, but my good, my expected, monastic behaviour did not last for long.

The third was my lack of obedience and humility. For instance, I had been informed, by the Novice Master and then the Prior that I should no longer spend time with the two more senior monks with whom I had developed a friendship and with whom I discussed all manner of arcane matters.

Although I agreed to abide "by the rules" it was not long before I broke them, again.

My rather un-monastic attitude was not helped when I pinned the following on the cloister noticeboard:

> And Jesus said unto his disciples - "And who do you say that I am?"
>
> And they replied - " You are the eschatological manifestation of the ground of our being, the kerygma in which we find the ultimate meaning of our interpersonal relationships. "
>
> And Jesus looked at them amazed, and said, "*You what?*"

I cannot now remember where I obtained this quote from - some newly published book, perhaps - but my attempt at humour was somewhat unappreciated. My excuse? It had been suggested that we novices read Barth's *Church Dogmatics.*

Another incident - revealing of my nature - is perhaps worth recalling. An elderly monk died, peacefully, in his room, and on hearing this I rushed along the cloister to ring "the big bell", for I remembered having read somewhere (perhaps in the Rule of Saint Benedict) that what is what one should do, thus enabling the monks to pray for the soul of our departed brother. Naturally, I got into trouble for doing this - the bell could be heard for miles - for apparently this was, in that monastery, no longer the custom, and I should, of course, have asked permission first. Also, naturally, I argued the point - for a while, at least.

It was not that I made some sudden decision to leave. Rather, it became - after nearly a year and a half - rather obvious to me that I really did not have a vocation, a sentiment subsequently shared by both the Abbot and the Novice Master. Thus, by mutual consent, I eventually left, to return to live, for a while, in a caravan in the Fens.

The most poignant, the most remembered, thing about my leaving was when I went to tell the monk who had been a Zen Master, who said that of all the novices he had known in the past few years, I was the most monastic of them all. "This place needs people like you..." he said. But he was, to be fair, something of a character, himself, and had a wicked sense of humour.

Wandering, Love, and Marriage

During my last few months in the monastery, one of my given tasks had been to care for, to nurse, an elderly monk with a terminal disease, and - to my great surprise - the Abbot had occasion to thank me, several times, in person, for my work. Even so, he surprised me yet again by suggesting, on the day before my departure, that I should consider a career as a Nurse. Which I duly did and - with his letter of recommendation - managed to secure a place as a student Nurse. The start of the training course, however, was many months away, and so, for a while, I wandered around, once again, as an itinerant.

This wandering gave me time to reflect upon many things - especially my monastic life - and one thing I began to appreciate in a more conscious way was the centuries-long still living culture to which I belonged, of which Catholicism, monasticism, and Christianity in general, had been a part. For me, this was, and had been, especially manifest in two things: in plainchant (which I loved to sing and to listen to), and in classical music from medieval times to JS Bach, Haydn, and beyond, and a lot of which music - especially JS Bach and Haydn - was imbued with or inspired by a religious feeling, an appreciation and a knowing of the numinous.

This reflexion placed many things into a supra-personal perspective so that, for instance, I began to consider certain philosophical and ethical questions, including the nature of human love and human suffering, and the ethics of politics. During my time in the monastery I rarely thought about politics - or even about the world outside - and certainly did not miss political activity or involvement. I was far too occupied with daily monastic life and with my own studies, which included ancient Greek literature, Buddhism, Taoism and Western philosophy. These reflexions in turn led me to consider the nature and form of religion, especially in relation to Christian history and theology.

Thus my life became, for around three years after I had left the monastery, personal - for there was no involvements with politics, or even with any organized form of religion, Catholic or otherwise. I had no rôle, no aim beyond pursuing my interests - such as running, cycling and classical music - and was even gainfully employed, for a year, at least.

For my nursing course had started. In those days, the training was mostly practical, on the hospital wards, with a three month assignment on a certain type of ward (medical, surgical, and so on) followed by a few weeks back in the classroom, followed by another duty on another ward.

Sitting quietly in high Summer
While the river flows
Is peaceful, for an hour;
But any longer, and we who wish
Cannot wait to abstain:
We must be gone or find a goal
To satisfy such haste.

There was a man, dying from his age
As his flesh and organs failed:
He did not seem to mind this
        I've had a good innings
Except, sometimes, the pain.
He would lay, slowing breathing
And sometimes smiling in his bed
While we who waited on the living
And the dying
Cared
As our time, tiredness and allocations
Allowed.

Every two hours, on the Ward, still living bodies
Would be turned
To remove just one more soiled sheet
While the heat of Summer through half-open
Windows
Mingled with the smells
And the oozing from freshly sutured
Flesh:

But each dark moment was almost always
(If you watched)
Relieved
By the sadness or the smile
In another person's eyes.

And there was a learning
In such simple glimpses,
Shared.

I was one of only two male nurses on the course, and while the work itself was quite tiring and hard - and one went through periods of loving it, hating it, loving it - it was rewarding, and there was a sense, in those days, of belonging to a small community, especially since I lived, in a minuscule room, in the Nurses Home. One lived and worked in the same place, and generally spent time off-duty with one's fellow student nurses, in one's own year or from other years.

Naturally, there were liaisons with people with whom one worked and who also lived within the hospital grounds, and after a few of these I found myself in a serious relationship. There were plans for us to obtain our own accommodation, near the hospital; short holidays, away; and I felt I was in love. The young lady in question certainly was in love with me. But then, as my first year moved toward its ending, I - stupidly, selfishly, dishonourably - ruined it all, by falling in love with someone else.

The "other woman" was a friend of a friend, and then a Post Graduate studying at Cambridge, whom I met at some party or other in that city. Her nickname was Twinkle, and there was a quite adorable child-like quality to her, a need to be loved, an enthusiasm tempered occasionally by a touch of anxiety, all of which, combined with a keen intellect and a love of classical music, poetry and English literature, made her (at least to me) irresistible. I did try to resist - for a while. For several months, I managed to behave honourably, and even managed to behave in a friendly way toward her then lover. But the more I saw of her, the worse I felt.

For weeks, I resisted the temptation to see her, and was glad when she moved away, her course over, to live and work in what seemed far off Shropshire. But then her fateful short note arrived in the post - "Feeling wretched. Do come!" it read, giving a telephone number and an address. The very next day another, quite similar, note arrived, sounding even more urgent.

Making excuses to K - for I was genuinely concerned Twinkle might harm herself - I set off, without any expectations and rather naively believing I could be a good friend. A train to Shrewsbury; a bus to that overgrown village where she lived where once there was a medieval Priory; and there she was, waiting for me at the bus stop. Alighting from the bus, she ran to embrace me, and clung onto me for what seemed, what felt, a long time. "I wish I had a camera!" an elderly lady, waiting at the stop said, and smiled. And then we were walking, rather shyly together, along the road to her lodgings.

Hours later, the evening meal she had cooked eaten, we sat - she on a chair, I on the carpet before the gas fire - in her room in the candlelit dark while she, to a mute background of a symphony by Brahms - tearfully recalled the last few weeks of her life. Her lover had spurned her, harshly, for someone else;

she felt so alone; so betrayed; so ashamed of herself; so disgusted with herself for being so weak and needy, believing she was unworthy of being loved...

What could I say? Do? I should have played the rôle of unworldly, detached, Sage, and spake forth some words of fatherly wisdom and advice - but all I did in my weakness was move toward her, hold her hand and told her that I loved her. Thus did I that night and the next betray my lover. K met me at the railway station on my return, and she knew, just knew, immediately, of my betrayal, just as I felt her knowing. We did not speak of it then, and strived to carry on as normal, until some days later when a letter for me from Twinkle arrived. I was on duty, and K opened and read it. There were no tears from her on my return to my room in the Nurses Home; no words shouted; no words at all. She simply gave me the letter and waited. There was, in that letter, a declaration of love, a passage about having children - about how even now she might be bearing "our child".

There were tears from she whom I had betrayed, and I felt ashamed, and the most wretched I had ever, up until then, felt in my life. Wretched because of her sadness, her feelings; wretched because I had so deeply hurt her; and wretched because there was no anger in her, no words or shouts of recrimination; no accusations; no flailing fists of a lover betrayed. Only deep soul-wrenching almost utter despair. She left then to leave me alone with my dishonour, my shame.

A few days later, I suddenly withdrew from the nursing course to travel to Shropshire to live with my new lover. The day before I left I had met K, briefly - or rather, she had saught me out. We embraced, then she pulled away to affect a smile while I just stood there, not knowing, in my shame, what to say or do. But she was far stronger than I and suggested, gently, affectionately, that - if I did indeed love Twinkle - then I could obtain a transfer to a hospital in Shropshire. She had it all worked out, having even spoken to a senior member of the teaching staff about such transfers. She left then, leaving me as if I had just awoken from some dream. A walk. Another walk. A telephone call some hours later; a question impetuously asked; an affirmative answer received. Yes, she would marry me...

I went to tell K. She had just returned from a late shift and, then as now, I am not quite sure how or why we parted in the gentle way we did. We spoke for a while, softly, of our own future separate plans; we shared a bottle of wine; then we were in each others arms; and in the morning we kissed and I, with no words exchanged between us, left to begin my new life in the rural county of Shropshire. Less than six months later I was married, to Twinkle, and never saw or heard from K again.

Now, recalling those events, I feel that K perhaps loved me far more than I deserved, as I know I behaved dishonourably and assuredly hurt her deeply. There are no excuses for my behaviour, then; I was quite simply - and for all my idealistic talk of honour in my political years - just weak, dishonourable. I gave in to my dreams and my desires, placing my needs, my dreams, my hopes, my lust, before the feelings of someone who loved me and whom I should have treated in an honourable way. In brief, I was selfish, and really did not know what love was - what it meant and implied - despite all my philosophical reflexion on the matter and despite all my previous trysts and involvements.

A few weeks before my marriage, I went to visit my lady friend in London for the last time to inform her of my change of circumstances, and spent an exquisitely poignant weekend with her; feelings recalled some months later in bleak mid-Winter:

> Like memories, snow falls
> With no sound
> While I stand as Winter frosts
> My feet
> And a cold hand holds itself ready
> Near a pen:
>
> The birds, though starving, still sing
> Here where trees and snow seat themselves
> On hill
> And the slight breeze beings to break
> My piece of silence
> Down.
>
> Her love seemed only real
> With its loss.
>
> Above the trees, crows cawing
> As they swirl
> Within the cold

A Shropshire Tale

The seven years of my first marriage were all spent in South Shropshire, that rural part of that border English county that I came to love. For a few months, after our marriage, we lived in lodgings and then in a caravan on the edge of a field on a farm, and enjoyed a reasonably happy time, until the snows of Winter came. I liked living in the quiet solitude of the caravan with its wood-burning stove, while she did not.

One morning we awoke to find ourselves snowed in, and I had to crawl out of a caravan window to shovel snow away from the door so that she could decamp to the nearby shack, whose rotting wooden roof and walls provided some shelter and which enclosed our portable chemical toilet. She had, quite naturally, endured enough, and threatened that day to stay with friends whose central heating, indoor bathroom, and kitchen she somehow found enchanting, suggesting then that we immediately find somewhere else suitable for us to live.

After a while we did, a brief interlude of living in Shrewsbury town not really worth recalling. We found a glorious house on the edge of the Long Mynd overlooking the Stretton valley, and it was there - with Coalbrookedale fireplaces in almost every room - that we would spend most of our remaining married years together.

The years passed - or seemed to pass, for me - quite quickly. I, occupied with cycling, with daily runs on the Long Mynd, writing poetry, with researching and writing a book I called, somewhat pretentiously, *The Logic of History* [6], and sometimes with work; she occupied with her full-time employment, miles distant (she possessed a moped) and her small circle of friends.

Work, for me, like money, was incidental, while for her, her career was the main enthusiasm of her life, and something she did with excellence and élan, and a consummate and professional ease. Thus, we existed quite often in our separate worlds, our married life more a convenience than a sharing passion, a fault for which I alone was to blame.

For instance, for me, weekends were a time for long fifteen or twenty mile runs - or fifty to eighty mile cycle rides, or competing in bicycle Time Trials at club level [7] - with the remainder of the day spent relaxing, perhaps idly walking up the Burway, or listening to music. In contrast, she desired a rather more active social life, and on the few occasions I accepted some social invitation - an evening meal with some of her colleagues, for instance - I either, in my then still somewhat arrogant way, monopolized the conversion, or was disdainful and disinterested.

Thus, as might be gathered from this précis, I was rather selfish if not downright uncaring, although I did agree, much against my own desire, to her wish to delay having children, given her commitment to her career. It is perhaps not surprising that she, therefore, with her passionate needful nature saught to find a type of love elsewhere. Thus it was that she fell in love with another woman. Or rather, we both were attracted to the same married woman, except, for my wife, while a physical desire existed, she honourably did not act upon it, while I - yet again - allowed my desire to overwhelm me, and thus betrayed her.

Had I learned nothing from the torment, the grief, the sorrow, of only a few years ago? From my other act of dishonour? Yes - but only for a while. Yet again, there are no excuses for my failure. But, aged a few years past thirty, it would be the last time I allowed lust to overwhelm my honour.

Our marriage survived, for a while at least. She, though deeply hurt, forgave me in that loving way that many women often can. But, unsurprisingly, and correctly, she began to find fault with me, our marriage, aided by a loving, tender, relationship she developed with a younger women. A year later we separated, and then divorced - she to live in a University city with her young lover, and I to stay in Shropshire.

During the years of my first marriage, I remained inactive in practical street politics, although I did keep in touch with both CJ and John Tyndall, and wrote a few articles, which JT published in his *Spearhead* magazine, both under my own name, and under several pseudonyms. [8]

For a few years, after my marriage, I worked in a few different occupations - or none, since by then I had a small private income - travelled [9], and enjoyed various liaisons with women, none of which lasted for very long and several of which placed me on the other side of betrayal, which in itself proved to be valuable, if painful, personal learning experience:

> A bright quarter moon
> As I ran alone in the cold hours
> Along the sunken road that twists
> Between hill-valley and stream:
>
> There was a dream, in the night
> That woke me - a sadness
> To make me sit by the fire
> Then take me out, moon-seeing
> And running, to hear only my feet
> My breath - to smell only the coldness
> Of the still, silent air:

But no spell, no wish
Brought my distant lover to me
And I was left to run slowly
Back
And wait the long hours
To Dawn.

By the fire, I think of nothing
Except the warmth of my love
No longer needed.

Then, one day - and arranged through a mutual acquaintance - I had an assignation with another women. Reverting back to country type, I wore a tweed suit, my tweed overcoat, plus traditional English flat cap. We had arranged to meet outside a Wine Bar in Shrewsbury, and, as her close friend, A, was later to tell me in a letter, Sue immediately fell in love with me:

" When Sue first met you, I've never seen such instant love and attraction. I've never believed in love at first sight but I have to admit you and Sue seem to have been the exception that proved the rule..."

That evening we had a long leisurely meal in that Wine Bar, and had a quite marvellous time, for there was a lovely, and natural, affinity between us. We arranged to meet the following week, became lovers, and then began living together.

Quite simply, I adored her and fell deeply in love with her. She was practical (she designed and made many of her own clothes), uncomplicated, and we just fitted together exceptionally well, never arguing, and never even - not once - exchanging angry words.

As her friend, A, wrote in the aforementioned letter:

" She had a very deep and simple love for you which never wavered. You and Sue were privileged to have that kind of love..."

We shared everything; went everywhere together, including holidays abroad. Indeed, twice every year we travelled to Egypt, once to spend two weeks leisurely cruising down the Nile from Aswan to Cairo, one of the last of those two week trips, then, since Middle Egypt, around troubled Assyut, became closed to Nile cruise boats, following some attacks on Western tourists.

Indeed, I can remember, on that particular trip, that armed Policemen accompanied our boat for part of our journey, as we were often escorted, on some excursions, by other armed guards.

My life became settled, and I was immensely happy. I began translating ancient Greek literature: first, *Antigone* by Sophocles, followed by *Oedipus Tyrannus*.

Then, just over four years into our relationship, Sue became ill. She had developed cancer. Surgery, and radiotherapy followed, and she seemed to recover, so we went again to Egypt. We had just returned when she became quite ill, and required emergency admission into hospital.

There we were, in an isolation room - it was feared, because of her yellow-coloured eyes, that she might have hepatitis or have acquired some tropical disease - awaiting the results of various tests.

"I am so sorry," the quite young hospital Consultant informed us, "it is very serious..."

She had around six weeks to live. Her first words to me after he, a lovely sensitive man, had left: "I am glad we went to Egypt." Then she smiled: "At least I'll have time to sort everything out!"

Never once, during those few remaining weeks of her life did she complain, even though she was on quite a high dose of morphine for her pain. Never once was she sad, dejected. Instead, it was she who - unbelievingly - gave me strength and support. She was, in a quite literal way, remarkable. We stayed, for a week, with her mother and brother who, having the means, spent every Autumn and Winter in Spain in a house overlooking the Mediterranean sea [10]. Then, her health deteriorating, we left to return to England.

One incident, at Malaga airport, enraged me. She was by then in a wheelchair, and we had requested priority boarding which the airline had agreed to. As I pushed her in her wheelchair I heard one British woman, in the departure lounge, make a disgusting remark, doubting whether "that woman" really needed a wheelchair. Enraged, I was about to shout something vulgar in reply when Sue gently smiled, held my hand, and shook her head. She died just over a week later, one night in her sleep while I sat beside her.

For months afterwards I shut myself away, at first in a room at an hotel in Shropshire, and then in a chalet in the hotel grounds. I busied myself with completing my translation of *The Agamemnon* by Aeschylus and going for walks on the Long Mynd.

Translation, and those walks, became my life. I had no other aim and three months became many more. I do not now recall how many months I stayed there, reclusive in my world, but however long it was I endured until my translation was complete. I even took the radical step - on a few occasions when busy weekends were expected - of hiring the two chalets on either side of mine in order to be alone, at peace, as I had my own table in the hotel restaurant, set well away from the others.

The translation over, I found myself - or so I believed - almost recovered from the immediacy of her loss. Sue, organized, remarkable, to the end, had planned her leaving well, and one of the few things she insisted upon, in those final weeks, was that I should, must, have a life after her. So she had a friend find an exclusive agency that specialized in personal introductions, and their card was in that leather Filofax that Sue had given me as one of her departing gifts. For weeks, I ignored that card, making a whole variety of excuses. Then, remembering, and placing my pride aside for her sake, and using one of those new-fangled mobile telephones, I made a call. Suffice to say - some interviews over, one at the village home of one of the ladies who ran the agency - I was offered an introduction.

I arranged to meet J at the Feathers Hotel in Ludlow, and she, as I, was nervous. She was well-dressed, well-spoken, well-educated, and somewhat reminded me of the archetypal English Rose. We arranged another meeting, and then another, and so began a rather old-fashioned courtship, which pleased us both, and it was not long before I fell in love with her. Years later, she confided in me that she began to fall in love with me on what was our second assignation when, in Worcester, after an evening meal at a fine restaurant, I was, as a gentleman should, escorting her to where her car was parked when I, like some schoolboy, unthinkingly blurted out, having taken out my pocket watch: "Gosh! It's half past nine already! I haven't been up this late for absolutely ages..."

Thus, there came a time when it seemed apposite for me to propose marriage. So I invited her to spend a long weekend with me at a rather lovely hotel beside a lake in Wales where, rather nervously, I revealed everything about my past. A few months later we were married, and honeymooned in the Maldives.

Life was never simple again, after that. For I had returned to writing about National-Socialism, publishing my fourteen volume *National-Socialist Series*, which included works with titles such as *National-Socialism: Principles and Ideals*, and *The Revolutionary Holy War of National-Socialism*.

Why this return? To be honest, I cannot really remember. But I have more than a vague suspicion that Sue's death had affected me more than I, at the time, cared or even dared to admit. Something seemed to have departed from my life: a personal vision, a dream, perhaps, of us - of Sue and I - growing old together; of a life of contented sharing, where the world was only our life together. For we had a beautiful life and home - a detached house, in Shropshire, tastefully furnished by Sue (who had impeccable taste); I had a collection of five custom made bicycles (including two with frames hand-crafted by Mercian); we had relaxing enjoyable holidays several times a year; our relationship was everything I had ever dreamed about; we had no financial concerns; and we were totally loyal to each other. I was, quite simply, in love and content, as I knew she was.

So, perhaps I replaced my personal vision with another one, retreating back into the world I had known before. The world of NS politics; of striving to create a better world, for others, based on the values of honour, loyalty and duty. In some ways, these NS writings of mine were an attempt to not only express the essence of what I believed National-Socialism to be, but also to evolve it, and I began to circulate a small newsletter, *The National-Socialist*, in the hope of introducing these ideas of mine to others.

It was around this time that the London-based group Combat 18 was becoming well-known, and it seemed to me that many of those involved with this group were doing what I had again, and at that time, come to believe was necessary, which was revolutionary street-action in the name of National-Socialism, just as I believed then, as before, that I, by supporting NS, was doing something honourable and noble.

As I wrote in a previous autobiographical note, published in 1998:

> I came to admire them and openly declared my support for them. I also gave a personal pledge of loyalty to Combat 18's leader,

Charlie Sargent, and his brother, Steve.

In a short space of time Combat 18 had built up a fearsome reputation and done what no other group had done - gained street power from those opposed to National-Socialism. Not surprisingly, the Press, aided by MI5, began a campaign to discredit C18, as both MI5 and Special Branch saught to infiltrate and disrupt the organization.

In article after article, in letter after letter, in discussion after discussion, I warned of the danger and urged people to uphold the values of honour, loyalty and duty. I also urged them to consider that the best way forward was a proper National-Socialist organization and to forget plans and talk of an imminent armed insurrection, for - as I had discovered from practical experience - the time was not yet right for such plans: we needed the people first, properly motivated, in their thousands, and we had but dozens. But the poison of the State took effect. People in nationalist organizations began to believe the clever MI5 dis-information about C18 being a MI5 run group, created to disrupt the so-called 'nationalist cause'. Some nationalists even went so far as to describe Charlie and Steve as 'informers'. Perhaps MI5 were also successful in disrupting C18 itself, or perhaps it was only the result of the ego and disloyalty of one individual.

Whatever the first cause, open feuding broke out between the two C18 factions, resulting in one death, and the arrest for murder of Charlie Sargent and his loyal comrade Martin Cross. I was honour-bound to stay loyal to Charlie Sargent, and decided to form and lead the National-Socialist Movement to continue the work he had begun. As a result, a smear campaign against me began. Rumours of Occult involvement - never entirely absent thanks to a few dishonourable and cowardly individuals - increased. But I believed I could ignore them as I hoped others around me would ignore them and hold fast to honour, loyalty and duty.

The decision for me to come back into public prominence by forming and leading the NSM was easy, even though I knew what would happen with regard to rumours about me, and even though I never intended to stay for long as the leader, lacking as I did the qualities of leadership. Yet, secretly, in my heart, I yearned for a quiet rural life, working on a farm and undertaking Greek translations in my spare time.

However, the decision to form and lead the NSM was easy because

I felt it was my duty - I believed I was responsible for what had happened to Charlie as I believed that someone had to publicly support him. I was responsible because in truth I - the exponent of honour, loyalty and duty - should have done something to prevent the situation that arose. I should have tried to bring the factions together on the basis of duty to the Cause first and foremost. I even went to Charlie's committal proceedings, after he had been charged with murder, in the belief that matters could even at that late date be sorted out. For I had a somewhat naive belief that the opponents of Charlie would see reason, ignore MI5 dis-information, and agree to put loyalty and the Cause first.

But the more I found out about what had happened, and was happening, the more I knew there could be no compromise with those who had betrayed Charlie, particularly by giving evidence against him in Court. This betrayal by giving evidence in a Court of Law was totally unacceptable behaviour - totally dishonourable. For we National-Socialists regarded the State and its Institutions such as the Police as our enemies, as we believed we should settle any disputes among ourselves in our traditional warrior way through a fair fight or a duel. Moreover these people continued parroting MI5 dis-information, and accused both Charlie and Steve of being informers when the truth was that the leader of their faction was the biggest informer of all, helping as he did to convict Charlie and Martin and supporting as he did the State and its dishonourable laws. Twice we who were loyal to Charlie waited for this informer and his supporters to turn up to sort matters out with a fair fight, once at Chelmsford and once in north London - and twice they did not turn up. [11]

My involvement with Combat 18, and later the new NSM, was to have a deleterious affect on my marriage, especially as my wife did not share my political opinions. *Searchlight* devoted several pages of one issue of their magazine to me, complete with photographs, including one of me on the front cover, under the headline *The Most Evil Nazi in Britain*. As usual, their story was a mix of some truth, some lies, and some unproven allegations. That is, it was political propaganda, designed for a specific purpose. In another issue, dealing with the trial of Charlie Sargent, there was a photograph of me (perhaps it was on the first page, if my ageing memory is correct) walking toward the Court in Chelmsford beside the wife of Martin Cross.

This photograph - together with my many trips to London - made my wife suspicious and so we argued, at first about "other women," and then, gradually, about other matters. On one occasion I had to go to Northern Ireland, and she insisted that I telephoned her from there, which I did, as she insisted on calling me back to check the number so that she knew I was there and not somewhere else. But, during the whole of our relationship I was never disloyal to her, having learnt that lesson, at least.

Meanwhile, I took to working on a farm, near to where we then lived in a detached house in a village not far from Malvern, and it was at that house that one local Policeman, accompanied by six Detectives from SO12, Scotland Yard, came to call, early one morning in 1998, to arrest me. For nearly seven hours they searched the house, seizing my computers, files, and letters, and arrested me. I was taken to Malvern Police Station, whose officers seemed somewhat bemused by this invasion of Detectives from an elite unit based at Scotland Yard.

A few interrogations, a period locked in a cell, and many hours later, I was released, on condition that I reported on a regular basis to Charing Cross Police station in London. I made a point, during my first "interview", of thanking the Detectives for their professional behaviour during their search of my home - for they had indeed acted in a very professional and courteous manner toward us - and it was this, and my subsequent interviews with SO12 officers in London (and on one occasion, in Oxford) - and the professional attitude of the custody Sergeants and other Police officers I had occasion to then interact with - that made me revise my attitude toward the Police.

My wife seemed, somewhat strangely, to take this invasion of her home, and my arrest, quite calmly, and did not seem particularly perturbed when I would adhere to my bail conditions and travel to London. I, certainly, was unperturbed - although my trips to London, the reaction of many comrades to "the dawn raids", and the attitude of the Police officers involved, did lead me to begin to think seriously again about the tactics, and indeed the rather stark ideology, I had been pursuing.

For, for all my rhetoric, for all my revolutionary words, for all my personal effort and sacrifice, very little - if anything - of practical import had been achieved. Indeed, the situation within and exterior to the NSM, and what remained of Combat 18, was analogous to the NDFM; in truth, it was far far worse. There seemed to be little honour; even less genuine loyalty; and the usual spreading of malicious rumours and of gossip. Furthermore, few people - if any - were prepared to risk their lives or their liberty for the Cause they claimed they believed in.

Hard manual work, on the farm, was some recompense, and I seriously began to wonder why I bothered with practical politics at all. But, outwardly, I maintained my revolutionary persona - at least for some months. For a new strategy had occurred to me, and this was that a religion might be very useful, or at least some kind of religious approach. Previously, I had rather vaguely written about NS as some kind of religion - but no one was interested, and it was, I knew, impossible to intellectually conjure a new religion into existence.

Thus, and impressed as I was at the time by the actions of devout Muslims who were, or who seemed to be, prepared to sacrifice their lives for "their Cause", I began to seriously study Islam, initially more to see what I could learn from it and perhaps apply to that NS Cause I then still believed in.

ooo

Pathei-Mathos

Copeland, The Way of Al-Islam, and A New Beginning

During my time with Combat 18, I had returned to Egypt, and it was during this visit that I began to appreciate the difference between Arab nationalism, and Islam, for I talked to several Egyptians, and several Muslims, about their land, about Islam, about life in general. I liked the manners of these Muslims, their devotion to their faith, which included praying five times a day.

I returned to England to find bad-manners, arrogance, materialism, decadence, and for the first time in my life I felt somewhat out of place among my own people. But gradually, over the coming months, the feeling faded.

As I wrote in Part Six of *Ethos of Extremism*:

" There was no sudden decision to convert to Islam [in 1998]. Rather, it was the culmination of a process that began a decade earlier with travels in the Sahara Desert. During the decade before my conversion I regularly travelled abroad, with this travel including well-over a dozen visits to Egypt and a few visits to other lands where the majority of the population were Muslim.

Egypt, especially, enchanted me; and not because of the profundity of ancient monuments. Rather because of the people, their culture, and the land itself. How life, outside of Cairo, seemed to mostly cling to the Nile - small settlements, patches and strips of verdanity, beside the flowing water and hemmed in by dry desert. I loved the silence, the solitude, the heat, of the desert; the feeling of there being precariously balanced between life and death, dependant on carried water, food; the feeling of smallness, a minute and fragile speck of life; the vast panorama of sky. There was a purity there, human life in its essence, and it was so easy, so very easy, to feel in such a stark environment that there was, must be, a God, a Creator, who could decide if one lived or died.

Once, after a long trip into the Western Desert, I returned to Cairo to stay at some small quite run-down hotel: on one side, a Mosque, while not that far away on the other side was a night-club. A strange, quixotic, juxtaposition that seemed to capture something of the real modern Egypt. Of course, very early next morning the Adhaan from the mosque woke me. I did not mind. Indeed, I found it hauntingly beautiful and, strangely, not strange at all; as if it was some long-forgotten and happy memory, from childhood perhaps.

Once, I happened to be cycling from Cairo airport to the centre of the city as dawn broke, my route taking me past several Mosques. So timeless, so beautiful, the architecture, the minarets, framed by the rising sun...

Once, and many years before my conversion, I bought from a bookshop in Cairo a copy of the Quran containing the text in Arabic with a parallel English interpretation, and would occasionally read parts of it, and although I found several passages interesting, intriguing, I then had no desire, felt no need, to study Islam further. Similarly, the many friendly conversations I had with Egyptians during such travels - about their land, their culture, and occasionally about Islam - were for me just informative, only the interest of a curious outsider, and did not engender any desire to study such matters in detail.

However, all these experiences, of a decade and more, engendered in me a feeling which seemed to grow stronger year by year with every new trip. This was the feeling that somehow in some strange haunting way I belonged there, in such places, as part of such a culture. A feeling which caused me - some time after the tragic death of Sue (aged 39) from cancer in the early 1990's - to enrol on, and begin, an honours course in Arabic at a British university.

Thus, suffice to say that a decade of such travel brought a feeling of familiarity and resonance with Egypt, its people, its culture, that land, and with the Islam that suffused it, so that when in the Summer of 1998 I seriously began to study Islam, to read Ahadith, Seerah, and the whole Quran, I had at least some context from practical experience. Furthermore, the more I studied Islam in England in those Summer months the more I felt, remembered, the sound of the beautiful Adhaan; remembered the desert - that ætherial purity, that sense of God, there; and remembered that haunting feeling of perhaps already belonging to such a culture, such a way of life. Hence my conversion to Islam, then, in September of that year, seemed somehow fated, wyrdful."

After some months of studying Islam, during that Summer of 1998 - my new strategy regarding some religion completely forgotten - it occurred to me that the Way of Al-Islam was indeed a good way to bring-into-being a new, a noble, society with a warrior ethos, and the more I read about the life of the Prophet, Muhammad, the more I came to admire him. There did, indeed, seem to be something remarkable, something numinous, something divine, here, in both the life of the Prophet, Muhammad, and in the Quran, and so – inspired and naively enthusiastic again - I trundled off to the nearest Mosque.

For nearly half an hour I hesitated - for these were the people I had spent thirty years trying to get out of Britain. How would they react to the former leader of the neo-nazi NSM walking into "their" Mosque?

At first when I, quite nervously, entered there seemed to be no one around. Out of respect, I removed my shoes and knocked on an inner door. The Imaam opened it - but he could not speak English, and I tried to say something in Arabic but the only thing that made sense was *Shahadah*. Soon, someone was fetched, who translated, and the Imaam embraced me. They were so pleased and so friendly that I admit that, then, tears came to my eyes, and I really felt I had, finally, arrived at the right place.

In retrospect, the years of my involvement with Islam were some of the most memorable of my life. Years when I learnt more about myself, and years which changed me fundamentally.

Not long after my conversion, I enrolled on a residential course in Arabic, and began to seriously study Ahadith, and, for several years, I was quite content as a Muslim - Namaz strengthened me, placed me into a humble relationship with my brothers and sisters; just as being part of the Ummah dissolved every last vestige of my former political beliefs. Ethnicity, one's territorial place of birth, the type of work one did, were all irrelevant. That is, I came to reject all forms of nationalism, including National-Socialism, and racialism itself.

I was welcomed into the homes of brothers, met their families, and there was this world within a world where what mattered was love of the prophet, Muhammad, and a desire to selflessly obey the word of Allah, as manifest in the Quran, the Sunnah, and *Ijmah*.

Meanwhile, my relationship with my wife became more and more strained - certainly not helped by my many absences to meet with Muslim friends, and most certainly not helped by the Media interest in me that occurred following the trial, and the conviction, of Copeland for the London nail-bombings.

Following the arrest of Copeland, I - by then a Muslim - was interviewed at my home by Detectives from the Anti-Terrorism branch who were investigating if I had any connection with him, and they seemed satisfied that I did not, for I was not interviewed again about the matter. Some time after this - many months, as the date for Copeland's trial came near - I was, for several days, followed around by a large red van which covertly filmed and photographed me, my place of work (a farm), and my home, before being waylaid, early one morning while on my way to work (as usual by bicycle) by a film crew from the BBC's Panorama television programme who were making what they described as a "documentary" about the bombings. Among the statements put to me that morning was:

"You inspired Copeland indirectly to do what he did.." [12]

Following Copeland's conviction and imprisonment, the BBC Panorama programme was broadcast, and I, not long after, was pursued for a while by journalists from several newspapers, with several scurrilous articles about me appearing in print. One even included a photograph of our house, and named the village where my wife and I lived. One of these newspaper articles began (complete with photograph of me riding my bicycle on my way back from work):

" *This is the man who shaped mind of a bomber; Cycling the lanes around Malvern, the mentor who drove David Copeland to kill...*

Riding a bicycle around his Worcestershire home town sporting a wizard-like beard and quirky dress-sense, the former monk could easily pass as a country eccentric or off-beat intellectual.

But behind David Myatt's studious exterior lies a more sinister character that has been at the forefront of extreme right-wing ideology in Britain since the mid-1960s. Myatt... was the brains behind the country's most openly neo-nazi organization....."

Yes indeed - *quirky dress sense*. That would be the type of clothes worn by a farm labourer, then.

As might be expected, all this Media interest somewhat affected my relationship with my wife, and she became quite distant, emotionally, physically, from me. Less than a year later, she became ill, suffering what is often termed a nervous breakdown. For a few months we stayed together, by which time it was obvious that our relationship was over.

In fairness to my wife, I have to admit that I had, yet again - and after my return to practical politics, followed by my conversion to Islam - descended down to abject, unforgivable, selfishness, placing some abstract goal, the personal pursuit of some abstract ideology, and then involvement with Islam, before her; before her needs. In brief, I was not a very good husband to her - more concerned with exterior supra-personal matters than with her, than with our relationship, than with her happiness. That she endured for so long with so little from me is tribute surely to her, as a loving woman. Mea Culpa, Mea Culpa, Mea Maxima Culpa.

Thus, my marriage over, I travelled in the Muslim world, met some very interesting and committed Muslims, all the while continuing my Muslim education, and it was some Muslims I met who asked me to write about this particular Way of Life; writings which I was, for some years, to become associated with, under my Muslim name of Abdul-Aziz ibn Myatt.

But was I, as some people have wondered, a sincere Muslim? Did I, for example, really believe that Muhammad was the Messenger and Prophet of Allah? Yes, I was sincere, and yes I did believe that, just as decades before, and for a while, I believed that Jesus of Nazareth was the Son of God. Did I really believe that Shariah was the best way of living? Yes - because I accepted that I was fallible, and that to submit to the will of Allah was my duty, my honourable duty, as a Muslim. [13]

In a literal way, Islam taught me humility, something I aspired to during my time as a monk but which my then prideful nature rebelled against.

Why, then, did I begin to have doubts about that particular Way of Life, as manifest in some effusions and personal letters I wrote? As usual with my life, there was no *satori* - no one sudden moment of enlightenment with one's life thereafter and always changed. Rather, there were moments of empathy, of greater understanding, of insight, followed by a gradual return to almost, but not quite, where one had been before. Then, after some causal Time - of a duration sometimes short, sometimes long - there followed more such moments, until a slow, almost alchemical, change occurred within.

In retrospect, this change had its genesis in three things. First, because practical experience - my life as a Muslim - revealed to me, after a few years, how even the Ummah was woefully divided, how some Muslims seemed to be Muslim in name only, like some Catholics obeyed the precepts of their faith if and when it suited them, and how, it seemed to me, the various interpretations of certain texts often led to adherence to particular abstractions over and above a living numinously. [14] Second, after several years of interior struggle, of dwelling upon certain ethical and philosophical questions, I came to certain conclusions; and third, because - and most importantly, most significant of all - I became involved with, fell in love with, a certain lady.

Thus, this drift away from Islam resulted from a strange - perhaps a wyrdful - combination of circumstances, and from one singular, important, event.

A Personal Tragedy

While still involved with Islam - although I had begun to develop my philosophy of the Numinous Way - I met a most beautiful lady. She was a friend of one of my closest friends, and he and his partner had, since the end of my marriage, been trying to bring us together, believing that we might find each other interesting.

By then, I had been living and working on a farm for several years (a life and a work which inspired that initial development of my 'numinous way'), and although I had had a few casual trysts during that time, I still nurtured a desire for a deeper, permanent, relationship, and - intrigued by what I had been informed was her love of the desert and her desire to undertake more such travels, especially in the Western Sahara, an area I had come to know reasonably well - I agreed to contact her, more with a vague kind of hope than any real expectation of such a relationship developing.

Thus, Frances and I arranged to meet, after speaking to each other, via the medium of the telephone, several times. I have always rather disliked the impersonal nature of that medium - for one cannot see the eyes, the face, of the person one is conversing with - but, rather strangely for me, I conversed with her in the days before our meeting for several hours, not once, but twice, for we did seem to have something of a rapport.

We met on the concourse of York railway station, and it would be something of an understatement to write that I was immediately attracted to her. In truth, I was rather astounded, for during our prior telephone conversations she had, several times, made it known to me that she was not "at her best", that she was still somewhat depressed, and that I was not "to expect too much".

Although I recognized her immediately, as she came through the crowd toward where I was sitting, I was so impressed by her beauty, her very presence, that, for several seconds, I quite literally could not move, and when I did, stumbling to my feet, she was there and, without hesitation, we embraced each other and kissed as though we had been lovers for months, years.

A day later, and I was already in love with her, and for almost a year I would - every fortnight or so and when possible - travel by train to visit her in York. In those days, such journeys and stays away were not onerous, for I had sufficient funds to travel First Class and stay in excellent hotels. Once - over the Christmas period - Fran came to stay at the farm, for nearly two weeks, and to write that we had an enjoyable time would be something of an exaggeration. By then, I had proposed marriage, which she had accepted, and then seemed unsure about. We talked during that time, at some length, about travelling - especially into the Sahara Desert, as we considered moving to live in Egypt, but never arrived at any conclusion.

For years before our meeting - for most of her adult life in truth - she had a difficult time caused by regular periods of clinical depression. She also, for some unfathomable reason, often disliked herself intensely. Yet she was beautiful - astonishingly so at times when life flowed within her and animated her - and intelligent and talented. But little I could say or do made her feel better about herself in those periods when she descended down into bouts of self-deprecation - at least, these things did not seem to work for very long. That is, she always and so sadly returned to such self-deprecation. Thus our relationship went from glorious, ecstatic, highs to tremendous lows. But I loved her, and so persevered, hoping, trusting, that such love would and could aid and help her. For I had glimpsed - in moments, and sometimes for days on end - the woman she really was, she could be, beyond her self-loathing, her sometimes self-destructive habits.

My diverse and interesting past did not help our relationship, for several of her friends in York had, without ever having met me, "warned her about me" and so perhaps confused her, somewhat.

After eighteen or so often turbulent months (during which time she was diagnosed with Type 1 diabetes), I went to visit her in her rather cramped flat in York, intending to stay only a few days. Our plan, then, was to find an apartment, possibly in York, or possibly even abroad, and so begin a new life together. A few days there together became a week, then two weeks, then three... for she did not want me to go and could not decide what she wanted to do. It became a difficult time, not helped by a full page article about me - complete with photograph - which appeared in *The Times* newspaper under the heading *Muslim Extremists in Britain*.

> " A neo-nazi whose ideas were said to be the inspiration for the
> man who let off a nail bomb in Central London in 1999 has
> converted to an extremist form of Islam...
>
> Myatt is reportedly the author of a fascist terrorist handbook and a
> former leader of the violent far-right group Combat 18..."

We or rather I talked, occasionally, about just impetuously leaving to begin new lives, together, in Egypt. For I felt such surroundings might gently entice her toward a new and better way of living which would enable her to find the personal happiness that so eluded her, except in moments.

But, after an intense six or so weeks in York, with still no decisions made, I felt that Fran and I needed a short break from each other. She did not feel this, and desired me to stay. But I - tired, physically, emotionally, and making excuses to myself - decided to go anyway, and so early one morning in late May I travelled back to the farm. Only hours after my leaving, she killed herself.

She left no note, had taken on overdose of insulin, placed a bag over her head and secured it with layers of tape, and it is true to say that I was never quite the same person after receiving that call from her mother, less than an hour after Fran had died and only hours after I had so selfishly returned to be again among, within, the rural peace of the farm.

For hours after that telephone call I could not speak, and wandered around the fields of the farm alone, dazed - as if all feeling, and most of my blood, had suddenly been drained away from me to leave me almost totally bereft of life. Then, alone again in my room, the tears came flooding forth - so many for so long I sank to the floor to rock slowly back and forth, as if all of Fran's suffering year after year was flooding through me, as if I was being tossed around by surging towering waves of grief and battered by storms of remorse. Then, thoughts of suicide. Thereupon a certain calmness as I began to ponder the best way to die - a shotgun, perhaps, barrels placed under chin...

So much emotion within me, so much grief, so much dark death-embracing despair at my own failure, my own selfishness, that I felt, I knew, I had to die, and I was on my way to collect the chosen instrument of my death when, perhaps fortuitously, my mobile telephone rang. I was about to turn it off but glanced at the screen to see who was calling. It was a call from her mother, and – then knowing this - for what seemed a long duration of causal Time (but was only a few seconds) I dithered between disconnecting the call and answering, intending to say a few brief words to express again my blame. Words of blame won, and so I answered her call.

But there was such sadness in her voice, such grief at the loss of her daughter, that I felt ashamed, utterly ashamed, of my own selfish self-absorption. Thus we talked, trying to understand the circumstances, and sharing a little of our grief. And as I listened to her words, her voice, there came upon me the feeling that perhaps I had to live, that I should live, in order to bear the shame, to feel my grief, to live with the knowledge of my selfish nature, my abject failure, day after day. That, surely, might be a fitting punishment, or the beginning thereof. To die might be easy; to live with such self-knowledge would surely be - and should be - hard.

My feelings at the time were weakly captured in an effusion, dated 30 May 2006, which I sent to a friend:

I know what I should have done - been more patient; more supportive; more loving; placing her feelings, her life, before my own. But I made excuses for my failings here, not knowing the depth of her despair even though I who loved her should have known this, felt this. I made excuses for my selfishness, and listened to her Doctor; to others; to my sometimes selfish desires, when I should have listened to her far more.

Thus do I feel and now know my own stupidity for my arrogant, vain, belief that I could help, assist, change what was. No blame for me, her relatives say - but I know my blame, my shame, my failure, here. Thus am I fully humbled by my own lack of insight; by my lack of knowing; by an understanding of my selfishness and my failure - knowing myself now for the ignorant, arrogant person I was, and am.

How hypocritical to teach, to preach, through writings, feeling as I do now the suffering of words, for she whom I loved killed herself only hours after I had left. Killed herself - only hours after I had left, despite her pleading for me to stay. There are no words to describe my blame; no words - for I had gone for a selfish break, to walk in the fields of the Farm.

So I am lost, bereft; guilty, crying, mourning the loss of her beauty, her life, her love, Never again to hold her hand; to embrace her. Never again to share a smile; a peaceful moment; our dream of being together in our home. The fault is mine, and I have to carry this knowledge of unintentionally aiding the ending of a life, this burden, and the guilt, hoping, praying, that somehow, sometime, somewhere I can give some meaning to her life, and perhaps live without ever again causing any suffering to any living thing... I miss her so much, so deeply, my mind suffused with images of what I did and did not do and should have done. If only I had not gone - or gone back to sit with her in that small garden as she wished.....

I shall never be the same again, deeply knowing that I do not understand.

(In Memory of Frances, died Monday, May 29, 2006)

In the weeks, the months, following Fran's death, Islam became personally irrelevant to me, for as I wrote at the time, I felt it would have been just too easy for me to depend upon, to turn to, to rely on, Allah, on God - to have one's remorse removed by some belief in some possible redemption, to have one's mistakes, errors - "sins" - voided by some supra-personal means. To escape into prayer, Namaz. Can there be, I began to wonder, hope, redemption - some meaning in personal tragedy - without a Saviour's grace? Without God, Allah, prayer, Namaz, submission, sin, and faith?

Gradually, painfully slowly, I seemed to move toward some answers, often as as result of personal letters written to friends [15]. For the act of so writing - of trying to so express my feelings, my thoughts - seemed to aid the process of interior reflexion.

However, for a while at least, I maintained a public Muslim persona, stubbornly clinging as I did to some notion of duty; to the pledge of loyalty I had given on my conversion to Islam, a pledge I still then, and for some time afterwards, felt I was honour-bound to honour, and it would take me some eighteen months of an intense interior struggle, and further development of the ethics of my Numinous Way, before I resolved this very personal dilemma. [16]

°°°

The Numinous Way/Philosophy of Pathei-Mathos

A Debt of Honour

As a result of my new and intense interior struggles - promoted by Fran's death - there grew within me one uncomfortable truth from which even I with all my sophistry could not contrive to hide from myself, even though I tried, for a while.

The truth that I am indebted. That I have a debt of personal honour to both Fran and to Sue, who died - thirteen years apart - leaving me bereft of love, replete with sorrow, and somewhat perplexed. A debt to all those other women (such as K, and J, and Twinkle) who, over four decades, I have hurt in a personal way; a debt to the Cosmos itself for the suffering I have caused and inflicted through the unethical pursuit of abstractions.

A debt somehow and in some way - beyond a simple remembrance of them - to especially make the life and death of Sue and Fran worthwhile and full of meaning, as if their tragic early dying meant something to both me, and through my words, my deeds, to others. A debt of change, of learning - in me, so that from my pathei-mathos I might be, should be, a better person; presencing through words, living, thought, and deeds, that simple purity of life felt, touched, known, in those stark moments of the immediacy of their loss.

But this honour, I have so painfully discovered, is not the abstract honour of years, of decades, past that I in my arrogance and stupid adherence to and love of abstractions so foolishly believed in and upheld, being thus, becoming thus, as I was a cause of suffering. No; this instead is the essence of honour, founded in empathy; in an empathy with and thus a compassion for all life, sentient and otherwise. This is instead a being human; being in symbiosis with that-which is the essence of our humanity and which can, could and should, gently evolve us - far away from the primitive unempathic, uncompassionate, beings we have been, and unfortunately often still are; far away from the primitive unempathic, uncompassionate, often violent, person I had been, until recently.

A chance, an opportunity twice refused after Fran's death, when I - still then addicted to abstractions - continued to sally forth on their behalf, as if in some way such abstractions were alive, or could be brought to life or made to live if only I, and others, fought for them, sacrificed for them, suffered for them, and caused others to suffer.

But, as the third anniversary of Fran's suicide approached - amid the beauty and promise of one more English Spring - I became suffused again with tears, breaking forth from the sadness, the tragedy, the knowing, of my own unconscionable mistake. The mistake of forgetting; of distracting myself. Forgetting the sorrow, the grief, the pain born from the moments of their dying; distracting myself as I have been by immersing myself in such abstractions as gave me some rôle, some illusion of importance, to keep me occupied, arrogant, and vain: a debtor running away from his debt. A debtor making excuses for each new scheme and scam: an excuse for every hustle, delusion, and lie. For it was so easy - just so very easy - to continue to delude myself.

There are no excuses for this continued failure, this error, of mine, following Fran's death. No words which can hide the truth I tried to hide from myself for so long. The blame is mine, and mine alone. The blame for not immediately acting upon my own inner understanding.

For the reality of my past nine or so years is not that of some sudden life-changing revelation, but rather of a profound inner struggle whose genesis lay years before - in my experiences with and passion for women; in my time in a monastery; in my ever-growing love for Nature and my involvement with English rural life; in Sue's illness and her tragic death.

This intense struggle was akin to an addiction, and I an addict addicted to abstractions. A struggle between my empathy, my understanding, my pathei-mathos, and my life-long belief, itself an abstraction, that somehow in some way I could make a positive difference to the world and that such abstractions as I adhered to, or aided or advocated were or could be a beginning for a better world, and that to achieve this new world certain sacrifice were, unfortunately, necessary.

A struggle which gave rise to what became - refined, and extended, year after year - The Numinous Way, and which struggle was an interior war to change myself, to actually live, every year, every month, every week, every day, suffused with an empathic awareness and a desire not to cause suffering; the struggle to abandon abstractions.

For nine years or so this interior struggle wore me down, until it gradually faded away. It was akin to cycling up a long steep mountain climb in mist and drizzly rain, struggling on against one's aching body and against the desire to stop and rest; and not being able to see the end, the summit, of the climb. And then, slowly, the drizzle ceases, the mist begins to clear, the road becomes gradually less steep, and one is there - in warm bright sunshine nearing the summit of that climb, able to see the beautiful, the numinous, vista beyond, below, for the first time, and which vista after such an effort brings a restful interior peace, the silent tears of one person who feels their human insignificance compared to the mountains, the valleys below, the sky, the Sun, and the vast Cosmos beyond: the wyrdful nature of one fleeting delicate mortal microcosmic nexion which is one's own life.

The Silent Tears of My Unknowing

Thus, and at last, I ceased all involvement with Islam. In truth, I ceased involvement with everything; becoming only one still error-prone human being among billions. One human being who had no aim, no goals, who adhered to no abstractions - either his own or manufactured by others - but who instead just lived day after fleeting or slow day, and who occasionally would record, by some written words, some experience, some personal feeling, or the result of some Thought, manifest as a poem, perhaps, or some missive to a friend, or perhaps an article to elucidate some matter concerned with that Numinous Way [17] which, over those nine years of struggle,

represented both the silent tears of my unknowing and the results of my
πάθει μάθος [18].

As I was to write, not that long ago now, and while on a holiday:

> The moment of sublime knowing
> As clouds part above the Bay
> And the heat of Summer dries the spots of rain
> Still falling:
> I am, here, now, where dark clouds of thunder
> Have given way to blue
> Such that the tide, turning,
> Begins to break my vow of distance
> Down.
>
> A women, there, whose dog, disobeying,
> Splashes sea with sand until new interest
> Takes him where
> This bearded man of greying hair
> No longer reeks
> With sadness.
> Instead:
> The smile of joy when Sun of Summer
> Presents again this Paradise of Earth
> For I am only tears, falling

Thus, it is to Sue and Fran to whom I dedicate this work: they who
profoundly changed me, and to whom I owe so much. They who by a
remembrance of their love, their lives, their gifts, have finally, at last - after
so much arrogance and stupidity and weakness on my part - revealed to me
the most important truth concerning human life. Which is that a shared, a
loyal, love between two people is the most beautiful, the most numinous, the
most valuable thing of all.

Fini

ooooooo

Footnotes:

[1] See also the section *Excursus - Galactic Imperium,* below.

[2] One thing about school Physics I continued to immensely joy was practical work in the laboratory, for which work I almost always received an A plus. Indeed, on the one occasion I recall receiving a miserly plain A, I complained about the marking.

[3] One humorous thing about this criminal trial - which lasted many days - was that I was "in the dock" along with some of our Red opponents. These so-called communists had all attired themselves in suits and ties and had short hair - in order to try and make a good impression - while I, *au contraire*, did not care to pander to expectations, and so had grown a beard, had long hair, sported jeans, a collarless shirt without a tie, and wore an ex-RAF Greatcoat. Thus, I somewhat resembled the archetypal communist agitator while they resembled archetypal fascists.

I was to keep this bearded appearance for the next thirty years, although I did, on occasion, shave off my beard if I needed to travel somewhere incognito, often using some alternative identity.

[4] Morrison was, in later years, to pen his own recollections of those violent times; recollections which were somewhat inaccurate. See the Appendix of *Ethos of Extremism* for my comments on Morrison's recollections of those times.

[5] In previous years, having an alternate identity or two proved useful, given my life-style and inclinations.

[6] An extract from this unpublished and incomplete work - whose manuscript I subsequently lost - was published, in 1984, under the title *Vindex - Destiny of The West.*

[7] I mostly rode a fixed gear bike, and never won any events, although I was second and third a few times. I just enjoyed the challenge, but did manage 50 miles in under two and half hours, and - a few years later - won my club's Best All-Rounder trophy, one year, for the most consistent rider during a season.

[8] One curious incident during these years - relating to politics - may be

worth recording. Understandably, given my extremism, the anti-fascist group *Searchlight* had taken a dislike to me, and - following the murder, in Shropshire, of the elderly CND activist Hilda Murrell, they gave my name to the Police as a possible suspect.

As a result, Detectives from Shrewsbury Police interviewed me both at my home, in Church Stretton, and my then place of work - a country house in South Shropshire. Satisfied with my alibi, they eliminated me from their enquiries.

I was subsequently contacted and interviewed by Jenny Rathbone, a rather attractive research assistant from ITV's *World In Action* television programme who were producing a documentary about the murder. She also seemed satisfied that I had nothing to do with the incident, and I do recall sending her, anonymously, a bunch of red roses with a card which read "Good luck with your investigations." It was signed, *A Little Devil.*

[9] These travels included various trips to Egypt, and two into the Sahara desert on a bicycle. Given that most of the desert area I explored was *hamada* - and thus did not have large, archetypal, sand-dunes - these bicycle trips were was not as difficult as they might seem.

[10] We had to obtain a special and official permit to enable us to take several weeks supply of heroin medication out of the country, as we had to obtain special medical insurance, both of which were very kindly arranged by our local GP.

[11] In his book, *Homeland: Into a World of Hate*, the journalist Nick Ryan made several accusations about me as well as published some rumours about me without providing my side of the story. For instance, he states:

> "When Myatt later falls out with Will Browning, he insists on a
> duel... I'm told he backed down when The Beast claims the right to
> use baseball bats as weapon."

The truth is that Browning - through a contact, and via e-mail - did suggest such a weapon, to which I replied that the only weapons which could be honourably used were deadly weapons, such as swords or pistols. I included with my reply a copy of the Rules of Duelling, and re-affirmed my challenge to fight a duel using such deadly weapons. I received no reply, and was not contacted in any way by either Browning or his supporters.

[12] As is a common practice with recorded television programmes, some of my comments were edited out by the producers.

[13] This obedience was why I, as a Muslim, supported the people, and the policies, I did - because I believed those Muslims were correct, and acting in accord with the Will of Allah, and because I regarded those particular policies as correct, according to Quran and Sunnah.

[14] Rather naively, perhaps, I had somehow expected Islam to be different, and it began to occur to me, from direct personal experience, that all conventional religions, and Ways - however numinously they might presence part of The Numen - were in some or many ways unreasonable abstractions which human beings had to align themselves to and strive to be in accord with, and which quite often resulted in a particular attitude antithetical to empathy and *wu-wei*.

Some of these insights were expressed in works of mine such as *Religion, Empathy, and Pathei-Mathos: Essays and Letters Regarding Spirituality, Humility,* and *A Learning From Grief.*

[15] Some of these letters have been published, by JRW, in the second part of the collection entitled *David Wulstan Myatt: Selected Letters, Part One (2002-2008)*

[16] As I wrote in a footnote to one of my many scribblings:

> For almost four years - since Francine's suicide - I struggled with this dilemma of honour and duty, believing that it was my honourable duty to stubbornly adhere to the particular Way of Life I had embraced in the previous decade; and stubbornly adhere despite the conclusions of my own thinking regarding compassion and empathy, manifest as these conclusions were in the ethical, and non-racialist, Numinous Way that I had continued to develope. Thus did I during this period, and several times, publicly and in private re-affirm my commitment to that particular Way of Life, striving hard to forget my own answers, born from my thinking, my experiences, and especially from that personal tragedy, for surely these things were only a test, a trial, of my belief, my honour? Was it not therefore my duty to just humbly submit to الله, to thus acknowledge that my own thinking, my own conclusions based on experience, were flawed, the product of error and pride?
>
> But, to paraphrase TS Eliot, here I am now, in the middle way I have devised for myself, having had many years, often wasted, the years between two wars within myself -
>
> > Trying to use words, and every attempt
> > Is a wholly new start, and a different kind of failure.

Thus, I have declared a still rather shaky new truce, a compromise: based on a treaty where I have (re)defined personal honour as a practical manifestation of empathy, of the desire to cease to cause suffering to living-beings, with such empathy and the compassion deriving from it a guide to living that awareness of ourselves as but one nexion to all Life and to the Cosmos, and which awareness, which Cosmic perspective, expresses both our true human nature and the potential we possess to change ourselves into higher, more evolved, beings.

I would like to believe that this new truce I have manufactured will hold, but I have believed that before, and been mistaken, and even now it occurs to me that my theory of ethics, my new definition of honour, is just that: *mine*, and that I may be wrong. Yet my experiences - my feeling for, my empathy with, the numinous (manifest for instance in sublime music or in a mutual personal love) - tell me I can only live what I feel, I know, I empathize with, and this now is presenced in my developed Numinous Way.

During these years of interior reflexion, I studied, for several years, what was regarded as the interior way of Islam - that is, Sufism - in the hope that such a study might provide some guidance in respect of the ethical and philosophical questions, in relation to the Way of Al-Islam, which still perplexed and troubled me. However, this study just led me back to my own Philosophy of The Numen, and to develope it further.

[17] In the late Spring of 2012, I completely revised my 'numinous way' following a year-long period of reflexion; a refection that led me to re-express, in a more philosophical manner, the basic initial insights (2002-2006) and the personal pathei-mathos (2006-2011) that inspired that 'numinous way'; a re-expression contained in the two texts *Conspectus of The Philosophy of Pathei-Mathos* and Recuyle of *The Philosophy of Pathei-Mathos*. Thus the philosophy of πάθει μάθος (pathei-mathos) - as outlined in those two texts - is not only my own now completed weltanschauung, but also represents both the essence and the substance of what I have retained of the 'numinous way' I haphazardly and sporadically developed between 2002-2006 and then, after 2006, I increasingly felt compelled to develope in expiation, in search of answers, and in an effort to understand myself, my extremist pasts, and the suffering I finally came to realize I had caused.

[18]

Ζῆνα δέ τις προφρόνως ἐπινίκια κλάζων
τεύξεται φρενῶν τὸ πᾶν:

τὸν φρονεῖν βροτοὺς ὁδώ-
σαντα, τὸν **πάθει μάθος**
θέντα κυρίως ἔχειν.
στάζει δ᾽ ἔν θ᾽ ὕπνῳ πρὸ καρδίας
μνησιπήμων πόνος: καὶ παρ᾽ ἄ-
κοντας ἦλθε σωφρονεῖν.
δαιμόνων δέ που χάρις βίαιος
σέλμα σεμνὸν ἡμένων.

If anyone, from reasoning, exclaims loudly that victory of Zeus,
Then they have acquired an understanding of all these things;
Of he who guided mortals to reason,
Who laid down that this possesses authority:
'Learning from adversity'.

Even in sleep there trickles through the heart
The disabling recalling of the pain:
And wisdom arrives regardless of desire,
A favour from daimons
Who have taken the seats of honour, by force.

Aeschylus: Agamemnon (174-183) translated by DW Myatt

∘ ∘ ∘

Appendix 1

Pathei-Mathos – Genesis of My Unknowing

There are no excuses for my extremist past, for the suffering I caused to loved ones, to family, to friends, to those many more, those far more, 'unknown others' who were or who became the 'enemies' posited by some extremist ideology. No excuses because the extremism, the intolerance, the hatred, the violence, the inhumanity, the prejudice were mine; my responsibility, born from and expressive of my character; and because the discovery of, the learning of, the need to live, to regain, my humanity arose because of and from others and not because of me.

Thus what exposed my hubris - what for me broke down that certitude-of-knowing which extremism breeds and re-presents - was not something I did; not something I achieved; not something related to my character, my nature, at all. Instead, it was a gift offered to me by two others - the legacy left by their tragic early dying. That it took not one but two personal tragedies - some thirteen years apart - for me to accept and appreciate the gift of their love, their living, most surely reveals my failure, the hubris that for so long suffused me, and the strength and depth of my so lamentable extremism.

But the stark and uneasy truth is that I have no real, no definitive, answers for anyone, including myself. All I have now is a definite uncertitude of knowing, and certain feelings, some intuitions, some reflexions, a few certainly fallible suggestions arising mostly from reflexions concerning that, my lamentable, past, and thus - perhaps - just a scent, just a scent, of some understanding concerning some-things, perfumed as this understanding is with ineffable sadness.

For what I painfully, slowly, came to understand, via pathei-mathos, was the importance - the human necessity, the virtue - of love, and how love expresses or can express the numinous in the most sublime, the most human, way. Of how extremism (of whatever political or religious or ideological kind) places some abstraction, some ideation, some notion of duty to some ideation, before a personal love, before a knowing and an appreciation of the numinous. Thus does extremism - usurping such humanizing personal love - replace human love with an extreme, an unbalanced, an intemperate, passion for something abstract: some ideation, some ideal, some dogma, some 'victory', some-thing always supra-personal and always destructive of personal happiness, personal dreams, personal hopes; and always manifesting an impersonal harshness: the harshness of hatred, intolerance, certitude-of-knowing, unfairness, violence, prejudice.

Thus, instead of a natural and a human concern with what is local, personal and personally known, extremism breeds a desire to harshly interfere in the lives of others - personally unknown and personally distant - on the basis of such a hubriatic certitude-of-knowing that strife and suffering are inevitable. For there is in all extremists that stark lack of personal humility, that unbalance, that occurs when - as in all extremisms - what is masculous is emphasized and idealized and glorified to the detriment (internal, and external) of what is muliebral, and thus when some ideology or some dogma or some faith or some cause is given precedence over love and when loyalty to some manufactured abstraction is given precedence over loyalty to family, loved ones, friends.

For I have sensed that there are only changeable individual ways and individual fallible answers, born again and again via pathei-mathos and whose subtle scent - the wisdom - words can neither capture nor describe, even though we try and perhaps need to try, and try perhaps (as for me) as one hopeful needful act of a non-religious redemption.

Thus, and for instance, I sense - only sense - that peace (or the beginning thereof) might possibly just be not only the freedom from subsuming personal desires but also the freedom from striving for some supra-personal, abstract, impersonal, goal or goals. That is, a just-being, a flowing and a being-flowed. No subsuming concern with what-might-be or what-was. No lust for ideations; no quest for the violation of difference. Instead - a calmful waiting; just a listening, a seeing, a feeling, of what-is as those, as our, emanations of Life flow and change as they naturally flow and change, in, with, and beyond us: human, animal, of sea, soil, sky, Cosmos, and of Nature... But I am only dreaming, here in pathei-mathos-empathy-land where there is no past-present-future passing each of us with our future-past: only the numen presenced in each one of our so individual timeless human stories.

Yet, in that - this - other world, the scent of having understood remains, which is why I feel I now quite understand why, in the past, certain individuals disliked - even hated - me, given my decades of extremism: my advocacy of racism, fascism, holocaust denial, and National-Socialism, followed (after my conversion to Islam) by my support of bin Laden, the Taliban, and advocacy of 'suicide attacks'.

I also understand why - given my subversive agenda and my amoral willingness to use any tactic, from Occult honeytraps to terrorism, to undermine the society of the time as prelude to revolution - certain people have saught to discredit me by distributing and publishing certain allegations.

Furthermore, given my somewhat Promethean peregrinations - which included being a Catholic monk, a vagabond, a fanatical violent neo-nazi, a theoretician of terror, running a gang of thieves, studying Buddhism, Hinduism, Taoism; being a nurse, a farm worker, and supporter of Jihad - I expect many or most of those interested in or curious about my 'numinous way' and my recent mystical writings to be naturally suspicious of or doubtful about my reformation and my rejection of extremism.

Thus I harbour no resentment against individuals, or organizations, or groups, who over the past forty or so years have publicly and/or privately made negative or derogatory comments about me or published items making claims about me. Indeed, I now find myself in the rather curious situation of not only agreeing with some of my former political opponents on many matters, but also (perhaps) of understanding (and empathizing with) their motivation; a situation which led and which leads me to appreciate even more just how lamentable my extremism was and just how arrogant, selfish, wrong, and reprehensible, I as a person was, and how in many ways many of those former opponents were and are (*ex concesso*) better people than I ever was or am.

Which is one reason why I have written what I have recently written about extremism and my extremist past: so that perchance someone or some many may understand extremism, and its causes, better and thus be able to avoid the mistakes I made, avoid causing the suffering I caused; or be able to in some way more effectively counter or prevent such extremism in the future. And one reason - only one - why I henceforward must live in reclusion and *in silencio.*

May 2012

ooo

Appendix 2

Concerning The Development Of The Numinous Way

Background

What I term The Numinous Way, as a philosophy and as a way of life, was not the result of a few or many moments of inspiration striking close together in causal Time as measured by a terran-calendar and thus separated from each other by days, weeks, or even a few years.

Rather, it resulted from some nine years of reflexions, intuitions, and experiences, beginning in 2002 when - for quite a few months - I wandered as a vagabond in the hills and fells of Westmorland and lived in a tent, and during which time I communicated some of my musings, by means of handwritten letters, to a lady living in Oxford whom I had first met well over a decade before.

These musing concerned Nature, our place - as humans - in Nature and the Cosmos; the purpose, if any, of our lives; whether or not the five Aristotelian essentials gave a true understanding of the external world; and whether or not God, or Allah, or some sort of divinity or divinities, existed, and thus - if they did not - whence came mystical insight, knowledge, and understanding, and what value or validity, if any, did such mystical insight, knowledge, and understanding, possess.

During the previous thirty or more years I had occasional intuitions concerning, or feelings, regarding, Nature, divinity, the Cosmos, and 'the numinous'; insights and feelings which led me to study Taoism, Hellenic culture, Buddhism, the Catholic mystic tradition, and become a Catholic monk. Later on, such intuitions concerning the numinous - and travels in the Sahara Desert - led me to begin a serious study of Islam and were part of the process that led me to convert to that way of life.

But these intuitions, feelings - and the understanding and knowledge they engendered - were or always eventually became secondary to what, since around 1964, I had considered or felt was the purpose of my own life. This was to aid, to assist, in some way the exploration and the colonization of Outer Space, and it was enthusiasm for - the inspiration of - that ideal which led me to seriously study the science of Physics, and then to seek to find what type of society might be able to make that ideal a reality, a seeking initially aided by my study of and enthusiasm for Hellenic culture, a culture - manifest in Greek heroes such as Odysseus and in the warrior society home to the likes of the sons of Atreus - which I came to regard as the ideal prototype for this new society of new explorers and new heroes.

After considering, and then rejecting, the communist society of the Soviet Union [1], an intuition regarding National-Socialist Germany [2] led me to seriously study that society and National-Socialism, a study ended when I peremptorily concluded that I had indeed found the right type of modern society. Thus I became a National-Socialist, with my aim - the purpose of my life - being to aid the foundation of a new National-Socialist State as a prelude to the exploration and the colonization of Outer Space, and thus the creation of a Galactic Imperium, a new Galactic, or Cosmic, Reich.

As I wrote in part one of some autobiographical scribblings issued in 1998 and which were based on some writings of mine dating back to the 1970's:

> "It is the vision of a Galactic Empire which runs through my political life just as it is the quest to find and understand our human identity, and my own identity, and our relation to Nature, which runs through my personal and spiritual life, giving me the two aims which I consistently pursued since I was about thirteen years of age, regardless of where I was, what I was doing and how I was described by others or even by myself..."

For it was this aim of the exploration and the colonization of Outer Space, and my rather schoolboyish enthusiasm for it, which - together with the enjoyment of the struggle - inspired my fanaticism, my extremism, and which re-inspired me when, as sometimes occurred during my NS decades, my enthusiasm for politics, for a political revolution, waned, or when my intuitions, my feelings, concerning the numinous and my love of women - the dual inspiration for most of my poetry - became stronger than my political beliefs and my revolutionary fervour.

The aim, the purpose, this idealization, regarding Outer Space even partly motivated my study of and thence my conversion to Islam in 1998. For example, not long before that conversion, in an essay entitled *Foreseeing The Future*, I wrote:

> " I firmly believe that Islam has the potential to create not only a new civilization, governed according to reason, but also a new Empire which could take on and overthrow the established world-order dedicated as this world-order is to usury, decadence

and a god-less materialism [...] I also believe that a new Islamic Empire could create the Galactic Empire, or at least lay the foundations of it. Perhaps the first human colonies on another world will have as their flag the Islamic crescent, a flag inscribed with the words, in Arabic, In the Name of Allah, The Compassionate, The Merciful."

Thus, as when a National-Socialist, I dedicated myself to my 'new cause', to an ideal I idealistically carried in the headpiece of my head: the cause of Jihad, of disrupting existing societies as a prelude to manufacturing a new one. In this instance, a resurgent Khilafah.

As with National-Socialism, it was the ideal, the goal, the struggle, which was paramount, important; and I - like the extremist I was - hubriatically placed that goal, that ideal, that struggle for victory, before love, fairness, compassion, reason, and truth, and thus engendered and incited violence, hatred, and killing.

In addition, I always felt myself bound by honour to be loyal to either a cause, an ideology, or to certain individuals and so do the duty I had sworn by oath to do and be loyal to those I had sworn to be loyal to. Hence when doubts about my beliefs arose during my decades as a nazi I always had recourse to honour and so considered myself - even during my time as a monk - as a National-Socialist, albeit, when a monk, as a non-active one for whom there was ultimately no contradiction between the NS ethos and the ethos of a traditional Catholicism, for there was the Reichskonkordat and the agreement Pope Pius XII reached with Hitler.

During my Muslim years I felt bound by the oath of my Shahadah; an oath which negated my NS beliefs and led me to reject racism and nationalism, and embrace the multi-racialism of the Ummah; and which general oath, together (and importantly) with a personal oath sworn a few years after my conversion, would always - until 2009 - bring me back, or eventually cause me to drift back, to Islam and always remind me of the duty I felt I was, as a Muslim, honour-bound to do.

2002-2006

This drift back toward Islam is what occurred after my musings in 2002. I tried to forget them, a task made difficult when later that year I went to live on a farm and also work on another nearby farm. For that living and such work brought a deep personal contentment and further intuitions and feelings, and a burgeoning understanding, regarding the numinous, and especially concerning Nature; some of which intuitions and feelings I again communicated by means of handwritten letters, mostly to the aforementioned lady.

For a while I saught to find a synthesis, studied Sufism, but was unable to find any satisfactory answers, and thus began an interior struggle, a personal struggle I made some mention of in *Myngath*. A struggle, a conflict, between my own intuitions, insights, and burgeoning understanding - regarding the numinous and human beings - and the way of faith and belief; between what I felt was a more natural, a more numinous way, and the necessary belief in Allah, the Quran, the Sunnah that Islam, that being Muslim, required.

For a while, faith and belief and duty triumphed; then I wavered, and began to write in more detail about this still as yet unformed 'numinous way'. Then, yet again honour, duty, and loyalty triumphed - but only a while - for I chanced to meet and then fell in love with a most beautiful, non-Muslim, lady. And it was our relationship - but most of all her tragic death in May 2006 - that intensified my inner struggle and forced me to ask and then answer certain fundamental questions regarding my past and my own nature.

As I wrote at the time:

> " Thus do I feel and now know my own stupidity for my arrogant, vain, belief that I could help, assist, change what was [...] I know my blame, my shame, my failure, here. Thus am I fully humbled by my own lack of insight; by my lack of knowing; by an understanding of my selfishness and my failure - knowing myself now for the ignorant, arrogant person I was, and am. How hypocritical to teach, to preach, through writings, feeling as I do now the suffering of words."

I did not like the answers about myself that this tragedy forced me to find; indeed, I did not like myself and so, for a while, clung onto Islam, onto being Muslim; onto the way of faith, of God, of ignoring my own answers, my own feelings, my own intuitions. For there was - or so it then seemed - expiation, redemption, hope, and even some personal comfort, there. But this return to such surety just felt wrong, deeply wrong.

2006-2009

For there was, as I wrote in *Myngath*,

" ...one uncomfortable truth from which even I with all my sophistry could not contrive to hide from myself, even though I tried, for a while. The truth that I am indebted. That I have a debt of personal honour to both Fran and to Sue, who died - thirteen years apart - leaving me bereft of love, replete with sorrow, and somewhat perplexed. A debt to all those other women who, over four decades, I have hurt in a personal way; a debt to the Cosmos itself for the suffering I have caused and inflicted through the unethical pursuit of abstractions.

A debt somehow and in some way - beyond a simple remembrance of them - to especially make the life and death of Sue and Fran worthwhile and full of meaning, as if their tragic early dying meant something to both me, and through my words, my deeds, to others. A debt of change, of learning - in me, so that from my pathei-mathos I might be, should be, a better person; presencing through words, living, thought, and deeds, that simple purity of life felt, touched, known, in those stark moments of the immediacy of their loss.

But this honour, I have so painfully discovered, is not the abstract honour of years, of decades, past that I in my arrogance and stupid adherence to and love of abstractions so foolishly believed in and upheld, being thus, becoming thus, as I was a cause of suffering. No; this instead is the essence of honour, founded in empathy; in an empathy with and thus a compassion for all life, sentient and otherwise. This is instead a being human; being in symbiosis with that-which is the essence of our humanity and which can, could and should, gently evolve us - far away from the primitive unempathic, uncompassionate, beings we have been, and unfortunately often still are; far away from the primitive unempathic, uncompassionate, often violent, person I had been."

Thus I was prompted - forced - to continue to develop my understanding in what began to be and became my own 'numinous way' and which thus and finally and, in 2009 publicly, took me away from Islam and my life as a Muslim.

Given that the essence of The Numinous Way is individual empathy, an individual understanding, the development of an individual judgement, and the living of an ethical way of life where there is an appreciation of the numinous, the more I reflected upon this 'numinous way' between 2011 and Spring 2012, the more I not only realized my mistakes, but also that it was necessary to remove, to excise, the detritus that had accumulated around the basic insights and the personal pathei-mathos that inspired me to develop that 'numinous way'. Mistakes and detritus because for some time, during the development of that 'numinous way', I was still in thrall to some abstractions, still thinking in terms of categories and opposites, and still fond of pontificating and generalizing, especially about The State [3]. I therefore began to re-express, in a more philosophical manner, the personal, the individual, the ontological, the ethical and spiritual nature, of The Numinous Way, and thus emphasized the virtues of humility, love, and of wu-wei - of balance, of tolerance, of non-interference, of individual interior (spiritual) reformation, of non-striving, of admitting one's own uncertitude of understanding and of knowing.

The year-long [2011-2012] process of refinement, correction, and reflexion resulted in me re-naming what remained of my 'numinous way' the 'philosophy of pathei-mathos', and which philosophy I attempted to outline in the two texts *Recuyle of the Philosophy of Pathei-Mathos* and *Summary of The Philosophy of Pathei-Mathos*, the latter of which was also published under the title *Conspectus of The Philosophy of Pathei-Mathos*.

As I mentioned in *Society, Politics, Social Reform, and Pathei-Mathos* [Part Four of *Reculye of the Philosophy of Pathei-Mathos*] -

"Given that the concern of the philosophy of pathei-mathos is the individual and their interior, their spiritual, life, and given that (due to the nature of empathy and pathei-mathos) there is respect for individual judgement, the philosophy of pathei-mathos is apolitical, and thus not concerned with such matters as the theory and practice of governance, nor with changing or reforming society by political means [...]

This means that there is no desire and no need to use any confrontational means to directly challenge and confront the authority of existing States since numinous reform and change is personal, individual, non-political, and not organized beyond a limited local level of people personally known. That is, it is of and involves individuals who are personally known to each other working together based on the understanding that it is inner, personal, change - in individuals, of their nature, their character - that is is the ethical, the numinous, way to solve such personal and social problems as exist and arise. That such inner change of necessity comes before any striving for outer change by whatever means, whether such means be termed or classified as political, social, economic, religious. That the only effective, long-lasting, change and reform is understood as the one that evolves human beings and thus changes what, in them, predisposes them, or inclines them toward, doing or what urges them to do, what is dishonourable, undignified, unfair, and uncompassionate.

In practice, this evolution means, in the individual, the cultivation and use of the faculty of empathy, and acquiring the personal virtues of compassion, honour, and love. Which means the inner reformation of individuals, as individuals.

Hence the basis for numinous social change and reform is aiding, helping, assisting individuals in a direct and personal manner, and in practical ways, with such help, assistance, and aid arising because we personally know or are personally concerned about or involved with those individuals or the situations those individuals find themselves in. In brief, being compassionate, empathic, understanding, sensitive, kind, and showing by personal example."

The Philosophy of Pathei-Mathos

It is the philosophy of pathei-mathos which represents my weltanschauung. For I now consider that most of my writings, my pontifications, concerning 'the numinous way' - written haphazardly between 2002 and Spring 2012 - are unhelpful; or of little account; or irrelevant; or hubriatic; or detract from or obscure the basic simplicity of my weltanschauung, a simplicity I have endeavoured to express in *Conspectus of The Philosophy of Pathei-Mathos.*

24th April 2012
(Revised November 2012)

Notes

[1] During this study of communism, in the 1960's, I began to learn Russian and would regularly listen to communist radio broadcasts such as those from Rundfunk der DDR,

something I continued to do for a while even after becoming a National-Socialist. Indeed, on one occasion I wrote a letter to Radio Berlin which, to my surprise, was read out with my questions answered.

[2] As I have mentioned elsewhere this intuition regarding the Third Reich arose as a result of me reading an account of the actions of Otto Ernst Remer in July of 1944. For I admired his honour and his loyalty and his commitment to the duty he had sworn an oath to do. Here, I felt, was a modern-day Greek hero.

[3] These un-numinous, errorful, hubriatic, pontifications about 'the state' included essays such as the January 2011 text *The Failure and Immoral Nature of The State* and the February 2011, text *A Brief Numinous View of Religion, Politics, and The State*.

Among the abstractions (categories) which needed to be excised from a supposedly abstraction-less and empathic numinous way were 'the clan' and 'homo hubris', a divisive category I hubriatically pontificated about in several essays.

o o o

Appendix 3

(Extracts from)
The Ethos of Extremism
Some Reflexions on Politics and A Fanatical Life

Part One: 1968-1973

Becoming Nazi

My practical involvement in right-wing extremist politics really began in 1968 when I, still at school and not long returned from a childhood in the Far East and colonial Africa, became an active supporter of the newly formed National Front and of Colin Jordan's newly formed British Movement. My initial motivation for joining these organizations and becoming politically active was simple: to further the cause of National-Socialism and to enjoy the comradeship, the struggle for power, and the violence.

Some time before becoming so involved, I had chanced upon a copy of Shirer's book *The Rise and Fall of the Third Reich* and was inspired by the described actions of Otto Ernst Remer during the July 1944 plot against Hitler. Familiar as I was with *The Iliad* and *The Odyssey* - with Hellenistic culture and history in general - I youthfully, rashly, made a connexion between the heroes of ancient Greece and Remer, impressed as I was by Remer's loyalty and sense of duty. This led me to, over subsequent months, read everything I could find about Hitler and the Third Reich; a reading which took me to local libraries and bookshops, then to bookshops and libraries in London. I even managed to find and buy copies (not originals) of old 8mm film of nazi rallies and some German propaganda films made during WW2, viewed using an old home projector; for I had discovered there was, even then in the 60's, something of an 'underground' market in nazi memorabilia.

Suffice to say that my reading and my viewing enthused me so that after a few months I considered myself a National-Socialist, an admirer of Adolf Hitler, believing that National-Socialism could create a new heroic age. To mark my 'conversion', I bought a small gold swastika tie-pin from a seller of nazi memorabilia and did not mind when, out wearing it, some people stared - for I was prepared either to launch into a rant about NS and Hitler or for a fight.

Thus while my initial motivation was naively idealistic and somewhat schoolboyish, I soon came to embrace NS racial doctrines, aided by acquiring and reading a copy of the English edition of HS Chamberlain's two volume work *The Foundations of the Nineteenth Century*. This meant I accepted that some races were superior, and others inferior; and that 'the Aryan race' - being the most superior, the most evolved - had a special 'destiny'. As for the extermination of the Jews, to be honest for some months I vacillated between two extremes - between believing 'it was unfortunate but perhaps necessary, an act of war' and between believing it 'was Allied propaganda'.

Horrid as acceptance of such genocide is, I had already become, without knowing it, an extremist; for I was prepared to accept or to dismiss horrid facts, certain truths, in the belief that what mattered was the goal, the ideal, and that to achieve this one had to be harsh, even fanatical and brutal. In addition, I had come to regard war - modern war - as necessary, as the breeding ground of arête, and in war people are killed or slaughtered, just as the victors, the Greek heroes, in the Trojan war slaughtered many of the people of Troy after its fall and just as Alexander decimated the people of Massaga.

Later on, I was to discover that I was far from being alone, in neo-nazi circles, in this detestable acceptance of brutality and genocide. For instance, I can recall several discussions about the extermination of the Jews with support being voiced for such measures, and several occasions when a certain song, well-known in neo-nazi circles in the 60's and 70's, was sung by 'comrades', with the song beginning "Gas 'em all, gas 'em all, the long, and the short and the tall..."

However, in the months following my 'conversion' to the cause of National-Socialism I could not quite shake-off - for all my new enthusiasm and fanaticism - certain uncomfortable moral feelings regarding the holocaust, and so began reading voraciously about the subject, a reading which included trawling through multi-volume accounts such as *The Trial of German Major War Criminals: Proceedings of the International Military Tribunal Sitting at Nuremberg, Germany*. But in the end, after months of such reading and study, there came a point when I simply accepted, out of a desire to believe, that the genocide 'was Allied propaganda' so that, to me then and subsequently, further research regarding, or rational debate about, the matter became unnecessary. In effect, I came to fanatically believe it was war propaganda, and this fanatical belief was immune to criticism as I became intolerant of, dismissive of, others who tried to convince me that the horrors of the camps were real.

In retrospect, I needed to believe it was propaganda, a myth, because to do otherwise would destroy the imaginary, the idealistic, the perfect, the romanticized, National-Socialism I then believed in and accepted. To do otherwise would mean that Hitler was not as I imagined him to be, as I hoped he was: a noble and good man who had triumphed against all the odds purely out of a love for his people and his land. Thus it might be correct to conclude that my research into the matter then was biased, born not out of a desire to find 'the truth' but from a need to prove that my own conclusions, assumptions, and beliefs, were correct. There might therefore have been an element of faith involved here, and subsequently, such that inconvenient, or awkward, facts and truths are ignored, dismissed, or regarded as the 'propaganda' of those opposed to one's beliefs.

Hatred, Love, and Violence

Although - on joining the NF and BM - I was very naive about politics, something of a tabula rasa, I soon developed the same prejudices and the same hatreds as the people I came to associate with; prejudices and hatreds aided by pamphlets and books read, loaned and given, and by discussions with party members, especially those belonging to BM. Thus I came to regard 'immigrants' as somewhat uncivilized, certainly inferior to White people, and considered their removal from 'our land', our country, as a necessity. Before this, I had no opinions, no views, about such matters, and my understanding of National-Socialism was greatly aided and developed by personal discussions with, and by written correspondence I had with, Colin Jordan.

During this formative period, I subscribed to items such as *The Thunderbolt* newspaper published by Edward R. Fields and so regularly received anti-Jewish and anti-Black reports; reports that seemed to confirm the necessity of racial separation and the need for a final solution to 'the Jewish problem'. For I had, in common with nearly all BM members and many NF members, come to believe that the Jews, in England, as in many other Western lands, had too much power and too much influence, were somehow by nature badly disposed toward White people, and thus were our mortal enemies.

In practice these beliefs and prejudices, this racism, meant three obvious things, and one interesting and curious thing, as least it is curious and interesting to me, now, on reflexion. The three things are:

> (1) That I developed a very idealized, a very romanticized, view of and naive love for those I regarded as my own people, my own race - especially in respect of English people; regarding them as probably the most civilized people on Earth who had built the best, the most noble, Empire the world had ever seen, and who had 'civilized' or brought civilization to large parts of the world.

> (2) That I developed a prejudice and antagonism toward other races in general, and in particular against 'Blacks' and Jews, and thus, as a group, and politically, hated them and did not wish to associate with them.

> (3) That I regarded violence in pursuit of my beliefs as natural and necessary, and came to regard political enemies - such as 'Reds' - as legitimate targets of political violence.

The one interesting and curious thing is:

> That despite my racism, my nazi beliefs and ideals, my political activism, I was not personally offensive to or prejudiced or violent toward or hated individuals of other races that I met, including Jews.

Thus, and apropos all four things, I somehow and in some way managed to compartmentalize my personal life and my political life, for although I enjoyed political brawls, and was not averse to using violence, it was not in my nature to be personally rude or offensive to or violent toward people as individuals, whatever their perceived ethnicity; unless, of course, they threatened me personally, one individual to another, or had personally threatened someone I cared about. In fact, my hatred and violence was more directed toward political enemies - especially during political confrontations - than it was to other races; so directed that for many years, from 1968 to 1974, I would actively seek out such potentially and hopefully violent political confrontations and enjoy them. This enjoyment, this seeking after violent confrontation, perhaps explains why Martin Webster, in 1971 after meeting with me a few times, described me to a friend of his (who was studying at the same University as me) as "having a death wish", a description which rather irked me then.

That said, about compartmentalization, I did for a long time - directly and indirectly - incite hatred and violence against other races, both by speeches, often vitriolic, impassioned, and always extempore, I gave at political events; in discussions with comrades and others; by means of articles I wrote, and by posters, leaflets, stickers, I designed. But this was, to me at the time, impersonal, just propaganda, somewhat calculated, and regarded as a necessity in order to achieve certain political goals - and was probably more reprehensible for so being impersonal and propagandistic.

Only on a few occasions was I directly, personally, involved in violence against ethnic minorities, and these were unplanned, spontaneous, incidents involving several 'ethnics', one of which incidents led to me being arrested and given a prison sentence, but in all of which incidents - to be honest - I was or became motivated by dislike of and anger at 'these foreigners' because I felt they did not belong in 'my country' and should 'go back to where they belonged'.

The particular racial incident that led to my arrest and my first term of imprisonment occurred in the early 1970's, following some racial clashes in Wakefield between skinheads and 'ethnics', in this instance people of or descended from those of Pakistani origin. On the day in question I, then domiciled in Leeds, was out with Eddy Morrison and a few other comrades handing out anti-immigration leaflets in Wakefield hoping to capitalize on the violence and so possibly gain some new recruits for the cause. The leafleting over, we came across a group of skinheads, some of whom I vaguely knew. Sensibly, Morrison left while I, sensing there might be - and hopeful there would be - some violence, went with the skinheads looking for trouble. Thus it would be fair to say that I was responsible for what followed, as the Judge at my subsequent criminal trial judged I was. Our group - these young lads and I - wandered around for a while until we found some young Pakistani men whom we racially abused and then began to throw stones and bricks at. They ran away, and we gave chase... Suffice to say, when this first skirmish was over, we - buoyed by our success and I seem to recall at my instigation - went off in search of more targets. Eventually, after perhaps an hour or so - maybe more, maybe less - we found ourselves the subject of a large Police operation with officers chasing us. We split up and I, not knowing the area, ended up on some industrial lot with several Police officers blocking the only escape route. Soon, the Police had caught and arrested all of us [...]

Part Two: 1973-1975

Ultra-Violence, Covert Action, and Terror

Two significant events during this period (1973-1975) helped shape and develope my extremism. One was that I was released from my first term of imprisonment for violence, and the second was that I was recruited by the underground paramilitary and neo-nazi organization Column 88.

Simply put, prison hardened me even more, while involvement with Column 88 confirmed my faith in the ultimate victory of National-Socialism.

My imprisonment had perhaps the opposite effect to what the Judge at my trial may have intended, for far from 'teaching me a lesson' it only served to make me more fanatical and more violent. It also enabled me to learn new skills and acquire new contacts of a decidedly criminal kind, skills and contacts which - as I have mentioned elsewhere - I put to use following my release when I formed a small gang of thieves to liberate certain goods and fence them in order, initially at least, to fund various political schemes and projects of mine.

In addition, prison life seemed to me to confirm two of the fundamental axioms of National-Socialism, that of the necessity and value of *kampf* and that of the *führerprinzip*. That is, of hardening one's self, being prepared to use force, to be ruthless, unsentimental, in order to survive and prosper; and either earning respect or being obedient and submissive. For prison seemed to be like some ancient uncultured, uncivilized, macho tribal society where force or the threat of force (by both cons and screws), and/or one's personal cunning, were the basis of life, and where those of a violent or of a cunning nature tended to prosper. Perhaps fortunately I was or could be both violent and cunning so it was not really surprising that I ran a racket inside, selling goods liberated from a variety of sources including prison stores.

This increased political fanaticism and more violent nature would lead me, months later and with the help of Eddy Morrison, to found, in December of 1973, a new political neo-nazi organization based in Leeds; the rather grandly named National Democratic Freedom Movement, and which organization would be rather aptly described, some years later, by John Tyndall in the following terms:

> " The National Democratic Freedom Movement made little attempt to engage in serious politics but concentrated its activities mainly upon acts of violence against its opponents. [...] Before very long the NDFM had degenerated into nothing more than a criminal gang."

Thus 1973 and especially 1974 became, for me, a time of ultra-violence, criminality, and of a fanaticism even more extreme than that of previous years. A period during which I was regularly involved in fights and brawls, regularly arrested and appeared 'in the dock' - including for running that gang of thieves - and which period would end, perhaps inevitably, with me being sent to prison for a third time.

" Among the highlights of that NDFM year, for me, were the following. I smashed up (with one other NDFM member) an anti-apartheid exhibition, in Leeds (twice). I gave vitriolic extempore speeches at public meetings (some of which ended in violence when our opponents attacked). I waded into some Trade Union march or other, thumped a few people then stole and set fire to one of their banners (arrested, again). I arranged a meeting at Chapeltown, in Leeds (the heart of the Black community then) at which only five of us turned up, including Andrew Brons but not including Morrison. We faced a rather angry crowd of several hundred people, who threw bricks, stones, whatever, at us, and we few walked calmly right through them to our parked vehicles, and rather sedately drove away, our point made. No one said we could do it.

I spoke extempore at Speakers Corner in Hyde Park for around a half an hour to a crowd of over a thousand; it ended in a brawl...Finally, toward the end of that Summer, a meeting we had arranged on Leeds Town Hall steps resulted in a mass brawl when the crowd of around a thousand attacked us, after I had harangued them for around half an hour. Several Police officers were injured as they tried to break up the fights. I was arrested (again) but soon was granted bail...

When my case came to trial, at Leeds Crown Court, I was accused of having "incited the crowd" and generally held responsible for most of the violence."

Everything I did in these years I justified to myself, and often to others, by invoking principles such as 'the survival of the fittest' and by the belief that in order to secure victory for the political cause I believed in, any and all means were justified, from violence to hatred to using rhetoric and propaganda in order to motivate people and gain recruits.

As for Column 88, involvement with that well-organised, now long-defunct, paramilitary group gave strength to my conviction that a National-Socialist victory was possible, for C88 had many overseas contacts, held regular meetings attended by young neo-nazis from all over Europe, and had among its British members not only many older professional people but also some members of the military. In addition, given its paramilitary nature and the paramilitary training undertaken, there was the knowledge that there were many others like me who were, under certain circumstances, prepared to use both physical and armed force in the service of our NS cause.

Thus I became aware that I and the few dedicated National-Socialists I had met in previous years in groups such as British Movement and the National Front were far from alone; that there were many other committed National-Socialists 'out there'. Which awareness, which practically acquired knowledge, not only strengthened my commitment to National-Socialism but which also strengthened my resolve to fight for 'the cause'.

There also developed in me during this time, and because of my involvement with C88, a realization that both covert action and terrorism were or might be useful tactics to employ in the struggle for victory, a struggle which I - extremist and fanatic that I was - accepted would be brutal, violent, and bloody, and thus possibly cost the lives of some of us, some of our opponents, and even some non-combatants. For I was during these years enthused and somewhat motivated by the rise to power of Hitler's NSDAP; a bloody, violent, struggle which had cost the lives of many comrades, from 'the fallen' of November 9th 1923 to Horst Wessel. I thus considered myself, and my comrades, as continuing that struggle - that struggle for the supremacy of the Aryan race, and the struggle against 'decadence' and our Communist, liberal, and Jewish enemies. In this struggle I personally - inspired by Savitri Devi's book *Lightning and The Sun* - considered the military defeat of The Third Reich, and the death of Adolf Hitler, as but temporary setbacks to be avenged.

In respect of covert action, I came to the conclusion, following some discussions with some C88 members, that two different types of covert groups, with different strategy and tactics, might be very useful in our struggle and thus aid us directly or aid whatever right-wing political party might serve as a cover for introducing NS policies or which could be used to advance our cause. These covert groups would not be paramilitary and thus would not resort to using armed force since that option was already covered, so far as I was then concerned, by C88.

The first type of covert group would essentially be a honeytrap [1], to attract non-political people who might be or who had the potential to be useful to the cause even if, or especially if, they had to be 'blackmailed' or persuaded into doing so at some future time. The second type of covert group would be devoted to establishing a small cadre of NS fanatics, of 'sleepers', to - when the time was right - be disruptive or generally subversive.

Nothing came of this second idea, and the few people I recruited during 1974 for the second group, migrated to help the first group, established the previous year. However, from the outset this first group was beset with problems for - in retrospect - two quite simple reasons, both down to me. First, my lack of leadership skills, and, second, the outer nature chosen for the group which was of a secret Occult group with the 'offer', the temptation, of sexual favours from female members in a ritualized Occult setting, with some of these female members being 'on the game' and associated with someone who was associated with my small gang of thieves.

While I enjoyed and then lived for political action - especially confrontation and brawls - and was motivated, fanatical, enough to speak extempore in public and take charge in a violent situations on the streets, and loved to plan such violence and motivate people to undertake it, I disliked the day-to-day organization and the (to me) petty manipulation that was, or seemed to me to be, the lot of an organizer and leader. I also lacked the charm, the charisma, the flexibility, a political organizer and leader needed.

In contrast to me, Eddy Morrison had a natural charisma, a certain charm, and was an experienced and adept organizer. He also, unlike me at the time, had a good sense of humour and was well-liked whereas I was probably more feared, or respected, because I was simply considered a nutter, a violent psycho. As a consequence, he was a natural leader; suited to leading the NDFM, and of all the people I knew at the time the most suited to organize and lead such a covert group especially given the fact that its ultimate purpose was to aid our NS cause. However, for all my attempts at persuasion he was uninterested in both C88 and in my ideas regarding covert action. He also, beyond being a fan of horror stories and of the fiction of HP Lovecraft, had no interest whatsoever in the Occult. Thus I had to make do with someone else as organizer and 'leader' of this covert group, this person - then a comrade, a married businessman living near Manchester - being the one who had suggested the outer, the Occult, form of the group.

For some time, this underground group appeared to flourish, with some 'respectable' people recruited - initially a lecturer, a solicitor, a teacher, among others - with some of the recruits becoming converts to or in some way helping our political cause, and with such clandestine recruitment aided, later on, by some unexpected, non-factual, unwanted, publicity.

But what happened was that, over time and under the guidance of its mentor, the Occult and especially the hedonistic aspects came to dominate over the political and subversive intent, with the *raisons d'etat* of blackmail and persuasion, of recruiting useful, respectable, people thus lost. Hence, while I still considered, then and for quite some time afterwards, that the basic idea of such a subversive group, such a honeytrap, was sound, I gradually lost interest in this particular immoral honeytrap project until another spell in prison for an assortment of offences took me away from Leeds and my life as a violent neo-nazi activist [...]

Birth of A Theoretician of Terror

It is perhaps fair to say - so far as I recall - that I was the one who, in C88, first broached the subject of using certain tactics such as improvised explosive devices and assassinations in a direct campaign against both our enemies and what I often then referred to as 'The System'. Prior to this - so far as I knew - training and discussions had been concerned with and were about possible future events, in particular a Soviet invasion of Western Europe, an invasion scenario which at that time (the early to middle 1970's, the Cold War era) was taken seriously by Western governments and Western military forces.

My basic idea - the plan - was to use such tactics to cause disruption, fear, and discontent, in order to provoke a revolutionary situation that our NS, our racist, our fascist, or anti-immigrant groups in general, might be able to take advantage of politically and otherwise; with part of this plan being to encourage the government to introduce more and more 'martial law' type control and regulations, which type of control and regulations (and surveillance) those in the military inclined toward a more authoritarian, or even fascist type, government might use to their advantage. For from such authoritarian or fascist type beginnings, National-Socialism might be covertly, gradually, introduced.

It needs to be remembered this was when 'the troubles' - armed conflict in Northern Ireland - was possibly at its most bloody, and which conflict, together with IRA attacks in mainland Britain, caused consternation and concern both in British government and in certain military circles, with some ordinary ranks, a few junior officers and even a one or two of the higher ranks covertly talking about a scenario when a military coup in Britain might be justified. Not that, so far as I with my limited knowledge know, this minority discontent among certain military - and perhaps a few intelligence - personnel ever become widely known or has even been mentioned in books, memoirs, or articles written about those times. But this discontent did capture a certain mood among certain people during that period, a mood I had some personal knowledge of, partly as a result of C88 contacts, partly as a result of some trips I made to Northern Ireland, and partly as result of other contacts such as squaddies involved with or supportive of right-wing groups.

Thus my ideas, my proposals, were to some extent grounded in the realities of those times. Times when disruptive industrial strikes and disputes were common in Britain, when the National Front could hold rallies and marches of thousands of people and had a membership possibly in excess of 10,000 members, when many more ordinary British citizens were, or seemed to be, generally supportive of the 'stop immigration, start repatriation' campaign, and when there was some support, or seemed to be some support, in certain military and even government circles for a more authoritarian approach to government.

I justified my ideas - the plan - and thus the use of such tactics by immorally believing and suggesting to others that in 'such dire times' victory could not be achieved without sacrifice and blood, and that for our people, our land, to survive and prosper it was necessary for some of us to be hard, ruthless; that 'history' showed that such ruthlessness was effective. And so on and so on. I do remember, on several occasions, idealizing the Roman Empire and ranting about how Rome built and maintained its Empire, its glory; not by negotiations, not by elections, not through a policy of peace and non-violence, but because ruthless men, hardened by war, had conquered, subdued and dealt severely with discontent and threats to 'the Roman way of life', to Rome, and to the Empire. Quite often I would quote some words of Hitler, from *Mein Kampf*, such as that the broad masses respond to what is strong and uncompromising; that a struggle on behalf of a weltanschauung has to be conducted by men of heroic spirit who are ready to sacrifice everything, and that if a people does not fight they do not deserve to live.

Hence, to me now, on reflexion, it does not seem to be hatred - of whatever type - that motivated those ideas, such a terrorist plan, of mine but rather a glorification of war, of strife; a belief in struggle, in 'the survival of the fittest'; a naive desire to personally act based on idealistic notions of sacrifice and glory, of being part of a desperate struggle, a war, that began with Hitler and the NSDAP. Most of all, perhaps, there was the misguided feeling that 'our people' were under attack, threatened with slavery and then extinction, so that desperate, ruthless, measures were necessary to save them. A feeling that most certainly derived from the absolute conviction I then had that 'race' - one's idealized race - was the most important thing, so that this idealized, mythical, 'race' came before everything, and therefore (so the perverted reasoning went) what was moral was what aided and ensured the survival and prosperity of this 'race'.

As for practical consequences, then, I do not believe there were any, of significance, known to me. For I discovered little support for these ideas, this plan, probably for a quite simple reason, which was that the people in C88 disposed toward and trained for action preferred to concentrate on C88's stated aims and objectives: of being a practical bulwark in the event of a

Soviet invasion or an internal Communist, extreme left-wing, revolution, and of slowly infiltrating National-Socialists into positions of influence within British society.

However, perhaps it was these ideas of mine, my enthusiasm for and rants about such action - to selected C88 people of course [2] - that later on resulted in a sort-of 'bomb making package' being produced by some of them (a package complete with several pairs of disposable surgical gloves), one of which packages was delivered to me, in Leeds, on my release from prison in 1976 but which I personally did not use given that shortly thereafter - for reasons outlined in *Myngath* - I, suffering from a loss of idealism, had a change of heart, and decided to become a monk in a Catholic monastery. A loss of idealism, a moral change, that would, however and unfortunately, not last that long.

Extracts from
Part Six: 1998-2002

Conversion to Islam

[...]
There was no sudden decision to convert to Islam. Rather, it was the culmination of a process that began a decade earlier with travels in the Sahara Desert. During the decade before my conversion I regularly travelled abroad, with this travel including well-over a dozen visits to Egypt and a few visits to other lands where the majority of the population were Muslim.

Egypt, especially, enchanted me; and not because of the profundity of ancient monuments. Rather because of the people, their culture, and the land itself. How life, outside of Cairo, seemed to mostly cling to the Nile - small settlements, patches and strips of verdanity, beside the flowing water and hemmed in by dry desert. I loved the silence, the solitude, the heat, of the desert; the feeling of there being precariously balanced between life and death, dependant on carried water, food; the feeling of smallness, a minute and fragile speck of life; the vast panorama of sky. There was a purity there, human life in its essence, and it was so easy, so very easy, to feel in such a stark environment that there was, must be, a God, a Creator, who could decide if one lived or died.

Once, after a long trip into the Western Desert, I returned to Cairo to stay at some small quite run-down hotel: on one side, a Mosque, while not that far away on the other side was a night-club. A strange, quixotic, juxtaposition that seemed to capture something of the real modern Egypt. Of course, very early next morning the Adhaan from the mosque woke me. I did not mind. Indeed, I found it hauntingly beautiful and, strangely, not strange at all; as if it was some long-forgotten and happy memory, from childhood perhaps.

Once, I happened to be cycling from Cairo airport to the centre of the city as dawn broke, my route taking me past several Mosques. So timeless, so beautiful, the architecture, the minarets, framed by the rising sun...

Once, and many years before my conversion, I bought from a bookshop in Cairo a copy of the Quran containing the text in Arabic with a parallel English interpretation, and would occasionally read parts of it, and although I found several passages interesting, intriguing, I then had no desire, felt no need, to study Islam further. Similarly, the many friendly conversations I had with Egyptians during such travels - about their land, their culture, and occasionally about Islam - were for me just informative, only the interest of a curious outsider, and did not engender any desire to study such matters in detail.

However, all these experiences, of a decade and more, engendered in me a feeling which seemed to grow stronger year by year with every new trip. This was the feeling that somehow in some strange haunting way I belonged there, in such places, as part of such a culture. A feeling which caused me - some time after the tragic death of Sue (aged 39) from cancer in the early 1990's - to enrol on, and begin, an honours course in Arabic at a British university [3].

Thus, suffice to say that a decade of such travel brought a feeling of familiarity and resonance with Egypt, its people, its culture, that land, and with the Islam that suffused it, so that when in the Summer of 1998 I seriously began to study Islam, to read Ahadith, Seerah, and the whole Quran, I had at least some context from practical experience. Furthermore, the more I studied Islam in England in those Summer months the more I felt, remembered, the sound of the beautiful Adhaan; remembered the desert - that aetherial purity, that sense of God, there; and remembered that haunting feeling of perhaps already belonging to such a culture, such a way of life.

Hence my conversion to Islam, then, in September of that year, seemed somehow fated, wyrdful.

Notes

[1] Honeytrap meaning 'something that is tempting' - as in the modern usage of honeypot - and

also something covert to attract/entrap a particular type of person. That is, a type of 'sting' operation. Thus, State-sponsored espionage is not implied.

This new life later on included entering the noviciate of a Catholic monastery, and which monastic experience led me to reform myself, at least in respect of immoral and criminal activities and thus in respect of involvement with such immoral honeytraps. However, this reformation then did not last, for as recounted here in Part Four, I had occasion, during the 1980's, to renew my association not only with some old C88 comrades but also with the mentor of that Occult honeytrap when, after of lapse of many years, I became involved again in neo-nazi politics and revived my project of using clandestine recruitment for 'the cause'. By this time, that Occult group had developed some useful contacts, especially in the academic world, so some friendly co-operation between us was agreed; a co-operation which continued, sporadically, until just before my conversion to Islam in 1998.

This clandestine recruitment of mine was for a small National-Socialist cadre which went by a variety of names, beginning with 'G7' (soon abandoned), then *The White Wolves* (c. 1993), and finally the *Aryan Resistance Movement* aka Aryan Liberation Army [qv. Part Five for details].

However, while some of these Occult contacts were, given their professions, occasionally useful 'to the cause' and to 'our people', by 1997 I had come to the conclusion that the problems such association with Occultism and occultists caused far outweighed the subversive advantages; a conclusion which led me to re-write and re-issue a much earlier article of mine entitled *Occultism and National-Socialism*, and which revised article was subsequently published in the compilation *Cosmic Reich* by Renaissance Press of New Zealand. As I wrote in that article - "National-Socialism and Occultism are fundamentally, and irretrievably, incompatible and opposed to each other."

By the Summer of 1998 I had abandoned not only such co-operation and contacts with such Occult groups but also such clandestine recruitment on behalf of National-Socialism, concentrating instead on my Reichsfolk group and my 'revised' non-racist version of National-Socialism which I called 'ethical National-Socialism'. Later still, following my conversion to Islam, I was to reject even this version of National-Socialism.

[2] I recall one occasion, early on, trying to discuss my ideas - the plan - with C88's organizer in his home while, at my suggestion, very loud military music was played, from a Hi-Fi system, in the hope that it might drown out any covert listening or recording devices. Since the reality was that we could not hear what the other person said, that particular silly ploy of mine was very quickly discontinued.

[3] I soon left that university however, for personal and practical reasons to do with a romantic involvement with a lady who lived hundreds of miles away.

Made in the USA
Las Vegas, NV
08 October 2024

96423391R10057